Lamps of Fire:
Studies in Christian Mysticism

Lamps of Fire

Studies in Christian Mysticism

Robert A. Herrera

INTRODUCTION BY
Frederick D. Wilhelmsen

ST. BEDE'S PUBLICATIONS
Petersham, Massachusetts

Nihil Obstat   M. Basil Pennington, OCSO
             Censor

Imprimatur   +Timothy J. Harrington
             Bishop of Worcester

January 9, 1986

The *Nihil Obstat* and *Imprimatur* are official declarations that a book is considered to be free of doctrinal and moral error. It is not implied that those who have granted the *Nihil Obstat* and *Imprimatur* necessarily agree with the contents, opinions or statements expressed.

LIBRARY OF CONGRESS CATALOGING IN PUBLICATION DATA

Herrera, Robert A.
  Lamps of fire.

  1. Mysticism—History.   I. Title.
BV5075.H47   1986   248.2'2   85-8242
ISBN 0-932506-40-2

St. Bede's Publications
P.O. Box 545
Petersham, Massachusetts 01366

Contents

Introduction

With pleasure I introduce this profound meditation by Professor Robert Herrera on four Christian mystics who have helped fashion the Christian sensibility and heart through a millennium and more of ecstasy, battle, rejection, triumph, indifference—and an unknown future. Selecting Pseudo-Denis, St. Bonaventure, Ramón Lull, and St. Teresa of Avila as peculiarly refulgent jewels within a brilliant history of Catholic mysticism, Dr. Herrera explores each figure within the context of his or her history, weighs contributions, tempers excessive enthusiasm and dismisses cynical rejection. I can think of no contemporary American philosopher better equipped to come to terms with the often confused and always convoluted history of the mystical tradition. Already a distinguished scholar whose work on St. John of the Cross and whose scholarly articles on St. Anselm of Canterbury have stamped his name with academic authority, Dr. Herrera was eminently the man to write the book that the reader now holds in his hands. Once he opens it, he will not be disappointed in what he finds.

Writing an introduction to an original study is often a temptation and always a challenge. Introductions to books are not book reviews. This is the temptation. Book reviews follow on and evaluate; introductions (here is the challenge!) precede and announce. I shall not evaluate or even indulge in the itch to engage in criticism, although I confess that I have little of the latter, in its negative mode, to offer. Let my introduction be a kind of *pregón* in the sense of the crier who promises what is to come.

Two traditions have dominated Western Christian intellectuality, the one finding its watershed in Plato as transfigured by St. Augustine and the other finding its source in Aristotle as purified and elevated by St. Thomas Aquinas. By no means negating the Aristotelian background to the mysticism of St. Thomas Aquinas and of St. John of the Cross (the author, as indicated, dedicated an earlier book to this disciple of St. Teresa), the book in question is located squarely within the tradition that finds its pagan origins in Plato and its Christian inspiration in the Bishop of Hippo. Discovering in Pseudo-Denis a curious and fascinating mingling of earlier Neoplatonic and thus pagan overtones with a Christian yearning for a God beyond all being and knowing in the justly famous "cloud of unknowing," Herrera concludes that the mysticism of Denis is basically intellectualistic, possibly never experienced by Denis himself on grounds justified by the principle of noncontradiction: had he been a mystic personally he could never have talked about the Union beyond all Being and Knowing with the Totally Unknown God. Nonetheless, the delphic and hidden history of the man who was probably a Syrian monk reflects admirably, by a kind of ironic analogy, his own doctrine. Unknown in his own history, his teaching leaves us in a blessed state of unknowing achieved, curiously enough, by a rigid withdrawal and negation of created things through an ascent that terminates in what Tillich might have called "The God Beyond God." But the withdrawal is intellectual, not really affective. The world is x-ed out but not erased. The Hierarchy of Being is *there,* but transcended.

The pervasive influence of Pseudo-Denis, according to the author, percolates throughout the whole Middle Ages bubbling in varying degrees of intensity, in the subsequent three mystics discussed in this book. Reading the immense figure of St. Bonaventure against the struggles interior to the new mendicant Order of St. Francis, the Seraphic Doctor emerges as a man who sought a balance, better yet a transcendence, of an arid Averroistic rationalism which momentarily seized power at the University of Paris and a kind of gnostic "enthusiasm" (one is reminded of Ronald Knox's book) by the Franciscan "spirituals" who would have leveled Christendom in the name of Joachim of Fiore's hallucinatory visions of a world purged of secular institutions, Church, and sacraments, in the name of a messianic rule by friars—the reign of the Spirit which prefigured modern secularist eschatology.

Bonaventure's tactic of moving from creatures captured in sensation and imagination to the soul as ultimately not only vestige or image but likeness of the Triune God, is prefigured by the Trinitarian structures he discovered in the whole symphony of being. The world as symbol, being as being more refractory of the Tri-Personal God than in being itself, is traced with delicacy in the text. St. Bonaventure's "Way" or "Journey" is understood as a "praying in thinking" which aims at transcending the thinking in a Love surpassing all earthly affection. And as the active St. Francis withdrew into his mountain on Mount Alverna, the poor man of Christ wounded by stigmata, as he called all God's creatures to sing the praises of their Lord, so too the soul in mystical transfiguration finds its home in Him. Bonaventure, in the delicate reading given him by our author, walks a tight and delicate and dangerous trapeze hovering over the pits of the new Averroistic rationalism and the quasi-hysterical visions of the Franciscan "spirituals." Even more, in the words of Dr. Herrera, Bonaventure "attempted to fuse the intellectualistic spirituality of Pseudo-Denis with the affective current and theological stance of the day."

We must not forget, if I be permitted a gloss, that the whole weight of the devotion to the Humanity of Christ, represented by all the poetry of Christmas and the Child in the manger, dates from St. Francis. Bonaventure was his voice. Open to maudlin sentimentality, the tradition has largely surmounted the temptation and has become part of the heritage of Western man. As Chesterton once put it, we bow down before the Child in Bethlehem as a child ourselves, but our simplicity of adoration is accompanied by the most dizzying of theological affirmations. In this we are knit into one. St. Bonaventure's journey from the world to God and from God back to God-in-the-world is more than a map; it is a promise and possibly a hope for modern man.

The extravagances of Ramón Lull seem to appeal to Professor Herrera. He treats them with a fondness possibly rooted in his own Catalan inheritance. The famous "art," that machine which prefigured the computer and influenced Leibniz, has been described as a "dial-a-dogma" apparatus and to my knowledge nobody has ever been able to reconstruct it despite the elaborate diagrams and instructions given us by Lull himself. But behind the geometrical dancing of calculations and the cross-filing of concepts with reality, there reposed, according to the author, two fundamental convictions: the need to discover an already pre-existent order in things and the need to see in this order divine love. Mysticism united with apostolic zeal, a zeal not quite tempered by an almost colossal failure in his host of enterprises; within the thought of Ramón Lull—that troubadour of the Lord— blazed the love of the Triune God. The Lover is fool, madman and jester, and a mystical ascent to God can even be kept alive in a world ravaged by Parmenidean *doxa*. Lull preached the technique of frequent ejaculatory prayers, a technique revived today in the Spanish-founded *Opus Dei*, as a kind of whip returning men to their origin in God. Typically medieval in his insistence on valor as the heart of all virtue, Lull emerges in these pages not as a religious crank but as a figure squarely within the broad sweep of Catholic mysticism.

The author culminates his study with St. Teresa of Avila and well he might do so. Confronting, with an expertise professionally his own, the charges of hysteria, Herrera locates St. Teresa within the Spain of Philip II, brooded over by the immense monastery-palace of the Escorial. Her sevenfold march to mystical union with the Beloved through the seven mansions of the soul was always influenced by the "two things necessary—love of God and neighbor." Standing at the crossroads between an old world then dying and a new world in the throes of childbirth, Teresa both repels the modern sensibility and seduces it by her immense common sense, her humor, and her thoroughly feminine personality. Herrera's description of the seven *moradas* is certainly the most delicate and precise writing found in his book. Balancing St. Teresa's metaphors against the meat of her thought, the author cuts to the heart of the matter when he notes that St. Teresa separates herself from the Dionysian tradition which always leaves the world behind and thus subtly deprecates the Humanity of Christ. This might work for angels, according to the Saint of Avila, but it does not work for men. In her own words, "everything here on earth . . . a tongue to help (the soul) praise him." God found in "pots and pans" is the same God captured in mystical rapture.

The reader will discover in this book two overarching convictions that seem to dominate Dr. Herrera's meditation: 1) Christian mysticism cannot be wrenched from its historical roots and must be read in terms of the historical soil from whence it was born. As this soil shifts from the desert and the early centuries of the Christian epoch to finally reach its apotheosis in the Spain of the Golden Age, so too do the configurations given the mystical spirit. Never reducible to that historical soil, always proliferating in highly individualized and strikingly unique men and women, mysticism is not a cloth woven out of one piece but a multi-colored cape blazing forth that unity in diversity which has always marked the Catholic spirit. 2) Mysticism remains for modern man a challenge to the highest aspirations of the human spirit, a largely unexplored possibility today for a world that has sickened within its own arid rationalism and secularism. An author commanding a vivid style, a sense for his lofty topic chastened by an awareness of the things that are, Dr. Herrera is to be thanked humbly for having given us this splendid book.

Frederick D. Wilhelmsen
Professor of Philosophy and Politics
University of Dallas, Irving, Texas

Lamps of Fire:
Studies in Christian Mysticism

Prologue

William James, with his usual acuity, noted that mysticism was an ambiguous term, often used as a reproach for opinions considered vague, vast and sentimental.[1] He believed the "door" to the mystical region to be the unconscious—in his vocabulary the transmarginal or subliminal—and accordingly considered its phenomena as closely related to psychopathology.[2] In spite of his distaste for asceticism and overly liberal use of the term "mystical" to include states produced by nitrous oxide, ether, and alcohol, his *Varieties of Religious Experience* present many subtle analyses which served to stimulate investigation in the field for several decades. James was right. The ambiguity of the term has caused a great deal of mischief, allowing a veritable host of *esoterica* from the merely weird to the downright pathological, to find sanctuary.

Many theological studies originating from Roman Catholic sources, such as Görres' *Mystik*, which parallel "divine" and "diabolical" mysticism, add to the reigning confusion. No wonder that philosophers from Xenophanes to Lord Russell have regarded mysticism as rather disreputable and inimical to thought. Although serious studies of the past half century or so have helped to restore the study of mysticism to a higher level, philosophy, remembering its ancient unsatisfactory relation with the hermetic tradition, has yet to accord it a cordial welcome. Although Rudolf Otto can speculate that mystical conceptions lie behind the higher speculations of modern times, behind the thought of Descartes, the occasionalists, Malebranche, Spinoza, Shaftesbury, Leibniz, and Kant,[3] this opinion has too much about it of a hasty generalization which philosophers would be loath to accept.

The Christian mystical tradition, not yet clearly distinguishable from the primarily ascetic bent of mind of the early Church, has its inception in the Christian Alexandrians, notably Origen and Clement, continuing with Evagrius Ponticus and Gregory of Nyssa, reaching a watershed with the *Mystical Theology* of Pseudo-Denis. This tradition is brought to the West in seminal form by Cassian, developed by Augustine, Gregory the Great, the Victorines, Bernard, Bonaventure, and many others, reaching out to Meister Eckhart, the Rhineland mystics, Teresa of Avila and John of the Cross. This very same tradition, no matter how muted, still influences spirituality today. But after the sixteenth century the literature of mysticism becomes, with few exceptions, either fantastic, parochial, or professorial. Perhaps because of this, contemporary man quite rightly senses that something has gone wrong—that the sacred has been lost or misplaced, that a new medium of access to the Divine must be discovered or a traditional one reopened.

At an early period, mysticism distinguished itself from theology proper by claiming to teach a deeper mystery. The "mystical" interpretation of Scripture proposed to unveil the hidden spiritual meaning of a text. Soon, the experiencing—the "tasting"—of this hidden truth was seen as comprising part of the process of assimilating its deeper meaning. It claimed to be a knowledge which transcended intellectual cognition and included a foretaste of the beatific vision itself. As this experience is ineffable, it can be compared to commonplace human experience only by means of analogy. Following the lead of Scripture tactile analogies abound.

The spiritual life has often been viewed as a journey which begins with the acceptance of Christ and ends in the beatific vision. Obviously, the mystical life has the same goal. However, it differs from the ordinary path in that here the presence of God is in some way experienced. The human condition remains its point of departure, spiritual and moral ascesis its method, and union with God the end in view, the desired homeland. The lower inclinations of sensibility are organized by means of asceticism to provide an "opening," as it were, to the free activity of God. Contact with God is experiential, at its highest point called ecstasy.

It is an accepted truism that the principle of all supernatural life is grace, itself usually imperceptible, as ordinarily it is given according to the measure of human nature. It is impossible to discern with certitude the supernatural element which is at work in the soul. The Catholic Church has been singularly ill-at-ease with any theory in which feeling is taken as the index of spiritual worth. (No one can feel the infusion or withdrawal of grace.) It is probable that it can reach its full development without going beyond this ordinary mode. The traditional division of the spiritual life into the ascetic and mystical takes this into account. While asceticism deals with the development of the supernatural life within the ordinary mode, mysticism deals with this life in a manner which transcends it. Both, in turn, are comprised by the traditional stages of purification, illumination, and union.

It must be admitted that many mystics would be hard put to find an appropriate slot in the complex diagrams given by theologians. William James points to the many saints and mystics which, from the modern point of view, are decidedly queer. Blessed Suso contriving new instruments of physical maceration, the dietetic practices of Peter of Alcantara, or the negligible practical talents of Margaret Mary Alacoque are scarcely in the modern temper. Still, they made sense to many of their contemporaries—albeit extravagant sense. Our own age can hardly plead innocent of bizarre behavior. Men and women go through tortures of mind and body to enter a crucible not unlike that of the mystics, if not for the sake of God, perhaps because of humanity, progress, economics, or just plain fad. How do we compare with the past? The prospect of such a comparison is hardly exhilarating. In any case, Margaret Mary in the kitchen was no worse than Woodrow Wilson at the map and far less dangerous.

Mysticism is certainly puzzling. A treatise of encyclopedic proportions might not suffice to unpuzzle it. But it should be kept in mind that its exotic language and all-attendant complexities hinge on one simple point. If God exists—a Christian accepts the premise—and the end of man is union with God through Christ, this union can be brought about by God as he wishes. The notion that the beatific vision is radically grounded in God—the *lumen gloriae* of the theologians— and not on man, delivered Christianity from becoming another priggish intellectual sect in which immortality is doled out in proportion to speculative genius. It prevented a relapse into a paganism lacking the grace of the hellenic bards or the fire of the hellenistic mystagogues.

The mystic is then the person who exemplifies divine generosity, who received the grace of God in an experiential manner.

Whether any of the "mystics" were imposters or even full-blown psychotics can only be left to the tender mercy of time and the judgment of the Church. A good dose of neurosis is not a decisive barrier to the grace of God. It is simply part of a personality which is to be restructured and transformed. The Christian saint has seldom subscribed to the Religion of Healthy-Mindedness. But the mystics might also be dismissed as otiose and of no utility to the human community. This objection could be countered by recalling that the worship of God is the first duty of man.

Nonetheless, the obscurity of the mystical writer, his hidden life, compounded with the many characteristics which simply do not make sense in the contemporary secular world, add to the impression that the mystic is at best a frightening monstrosity. It is not enough to mouth the pious truism that many great saints will be known only on the last day. It should be urged that mystical literature has contributed to the development of theological and philosophical speculation and, in the long run, to the constitution of worlds the mystics themselves would fail to recognize. The secular world of modernity has been shaped to a surprising extent by hidden forces.

In this small volume I have studied four mystical writers. Both biography and interpretation have a place. In some cases the mystic himself overshadows efforts at interpretation, although a rational coming to terms with mystical phenomena is attempted. In any event, there is a marked difference between those works which explicitly describe mystical experience, those with a pedagogical intent, and those which provide theoretical interpretations.[4] Although some theologians speak of mystical theology as a science—that is to say an organized body of knowledge—it should not be forgotten that if indeed it can pass muster as a science, this is due to the ossification of the original experience, and will remain at a distance from its force and immediacy. Rational speculation is then a safeguard against wild interpretation and not a revelation of mystery. Still, examining this privileged domain from the outside, as reason does, is usually the best that can be done.

The four mystics here considered: Pseudo-Denis, Bonaventure, Ramón Lull and Teresa of Avila,[5] are separated by time, style, and personality. Yet all four left their mark on Christian spirituality and exercised at least a tangential influence on the secular world. They helped to form the way in which Western man understands the inner world of spirit and the outer world of community. Our language, psychology and philosophy, our notions of self, time, and history, have been influenced by their thought. That posterity has, more often than not, accepted the rind of their thought and discarded the pulp is unfortunate though a muted compliment to their presence.

Pseudo-Denis presents the historian with many difficulties. In spite of the many hypotheses which have been framed he has yet to be identified. Scholarly consensus has him a Syrian monk, Neoplatonic in vision, living in the late fifth or early sixth century. His pseudonym and the biographical data given in his works gave him, with the passage of time, sub-apostolic authority as the Athenian convert of St. Paul. This awesome status served his works, the *Corpus Areopagiticum*, first in the Christian East where they were buttressed by the authority of Maximus the Confessor, and then in the Latin (Western) Church where it was translated, mulled over, and commented on with typical medieval rigor and imagination. The influence of these works on the intellectual formation of the Medieval West cannot be over-estimated. Even after the disintegration of Christendom they entered the modern world and the Dionysian presence is still recognizable in the major works of German Idealism.

Pseudo-Denis was able to provide mysticism with both a technical language and a theoretical framework, both grounded in Christian Neoplatonism. His vocabulary has shown remarkable powers of survival, fusing with later currents of spirituality. The theoretical framework came to lose its Neoplatonic emphasis due to the depredations of time and translators. A good case can be made that Meister Eckhart was the only thoroughgoing Dionysian after the tenth century. The influence of the *Corpus Areopagiticum* on Christian spirituality was immense, and figures as diverse as the Victorines, Bonaventure, the English author of *The Cloud of Unknowing*, and John of the Cross are greatly in its debt.

Denis' intense awareness of God's transcendence and his distaste for the material world is not in the modern temper. But many centuries were to take this attitude as a given. Although his tracing out of the angelic and ecclesiastical hierarchies strikes us as rather bizarre, it was based on the accepted belief that with Christianity the very structure of the heavenly court finds itself reflected in the constitution of earthly society. To structure the earthly city according to the blueprint of the heavenly city is imperative. The higher helps the lower to ascend to its proper place or level of spiritual reality. Anyone with aesthetic sensibility will admire Denis' superb use of nocturnal imagery to express spiritual reality, his ease in the invention of new words and startling expressions, and his forceful description of the human ascent to God. The belief that man is called to participate in Divinity is found in many religions, and Denis' insistence that God is found beyond the structures of the created world is still productive of speculation.

The ascent to God is undertaken by means of a definite method which involves a rigorous ascetic preparation. Its very point of departure requires a taxing effort of intellectual purification. Denis' seeming obsession with angels rests on the belief that they enjoy a close privileged relationship with both God and men, that through their help man is liberated from his bondage and is able to live an authentic life, straining to attain the fullness of divine likeness. The affirmative and negative ways associated with Pseudo-Denis, which have received much notoriety and perhaps not enough understanding, are basically ways in which man can evaluate himself vis-à-vis God. His overpowering sense of divine transcendence in which God is superior to being itself and hence No-thing is itself a way of coming to terms with the chasm which exists between the human mind with its categories and the God which not only transcends but overwhelms it.

In literature of the popular sort Bonaventure is usually coupled with St. Thomas Aquinas. Although this is somewhat misleading it can be used to point to several similarities. Both Aquinas and Bonaventure belonged to mendicant orders, taught at one time in Paris, defended the mendicant conception of poverty against the secular clergy, and struggled with the totalitarian rationalism of the Latin Averroists.

However, Bonaventure ranged further afield. As Minister-General of the Franciscan Order he had the delicate and well-nigh impossible task of reconciling the "Spirituals" while attacking their leader, John of Parma, his own immediate predecessor, as General. It was a nasty affair and Bonaventure did not emerge unsullied. The fracas was further complicated by the fact that most of the "Spirituals" were partisans of the Eternal Gospel, based on the allegorical interpretations of Scripture by the Abbot Joachim of Fiore which was popularized and modified by the Franciscan, Gerard of San Donnino. It became a heretical grotesque of great popularity.

As Abbot Joachim can reasonably be considered as a principal link on the chain between Augustine and Vico, setting the stage in some aspects for the later speculations of Hegel and Marx, the controversy surrounding the Eternal Gospel is still of some importance. Briefly put, Joachim interpreted history as a function of the Trinity. The era of the Father ended with the Incarnation, that of the Son which began with the Incarnation is presently coming to an end, and that of the Holy Spirit is about to begin. In this era the fullness of intelligence and truth would be manifest. A transformed Christianity composed of contemplatives will arise and the old hierarchical, sacramental Church will pass away. This utopian scheme is frankly and dangerously revolutionary, made immediately so by the belief current among "Spirituals" that Francis was the new prophet mentioned by Joachim and the Franciscans themselves the vanguard of the coming new order.

Bonaventure faced the challenge resolutely and probably did as well under the circumstances as was humanly possible. He also faced other enemies: the Latin Averroists, the proliferating wild religious sects, some of which like the Cathars were fundamentally alien to Christianity, the rising tide of Aristotelianism. He was still able to compose masterly works. His *Collationes in Hexaemeron* is a primary source for what has been called Christian metaphysics. Two of his works became classics of Christian spirituality, *De Triplici via* (The Three Paths) and the *Itinerarium Mentis in Deum* (The Journey of the Mind to God). Another curious work which deals with the relation of the spiritual life to the intellectual disciplines should also be mentioned:

De Reductione Artium ad Theologiam (The Reduction of the Arts to Theology). The title reflects the content.

The influence of Pseudo-Denis is very much in evidence. The notion of hierarchy plays an important role: earthly reality reflects the celestial hierarchy. The Church is viewed as organized according to the pattern of the heavenly Jerusalem and definitely not liable to any radical transformation along the lines preached by the Eternal Gospel. More in the spirit of Francis than his critics believed, Bonaventure's emotions are tempered by reason. Notwithstanding, the goal of his spiritual journey is infused contemplation which is characterized by affect, and its stages are allegorically represented by the wings of the Seraph who appeared to Francis on Mount Alverna. He adds a specifically Franciscan character to the literature of mysticism while attempting to curb the extravagances of the radical followers of the Poverello. In line with the early Augustinian tradition of which Anselm is probably the greatest example, Bonaventure sees the totality of human life as moving towards its completion in the knowledge of God through love.

If Bonaventure's life was characterized by constant struggle, that of Ramón Lull was one lengthy and supremely agitated pilgrimage. During his eighty-three years of life, Lull traveled through most of the known world and into those regions which had barely attained the status of legend in the Europe of his day. The extent of his travels remains a matter of scholarly conjecture. His youth seems to have been rather dissolute. As an old man he laments his weakness for female beauty. He is converted through the medium of several curious visions of Christ crucified and goes from being the *joglar* of many ladies— more than one the wife of a friend—to being the *joglar* of God. His exalted libido begins the difficult trek from sense to spirit. Lull's heated imagination, his feminine feel for color and form, hue and tone, led to a literary production of astonishing proportions. Any stay of a few months, sometimes less, during his wanderings, would produce a spate of writings of many different genres.

Another side of his character is reflected in his veritable obsession with logical method in the belief, perhaps inherited from Anselm, that a common ground in reason exists for all men, and to bring this ground to light could even bring about conversion. As Christianity dovetails with natural reason, it can make use of this common ground for apologetical purposes. The florid imagery of his literary works, populated by wise hermits, sage jesters, beautiful gardens, talking birds, and a multitude of other fictions, is in sharp contrast with the aridity of his geometric figures, key principles, and terms which undergird his famous Art. For nearly half a century Lull engaged in a veritable crusade to gain recognition. On February 10, 1310, a body of forty masters of the University of Paris issued a statement approving the *Ars Brevis*, a shortened exposition of the Art, as good, useful, and necessary. This is the best he ever obtained. On the whole, the Art was dismissed, along with its author, as a bizarre eccentricity.

To characterize Ramón Lull's passage through life as dramatic would be an understatement. Its feverish pitch, his many real and apocryphal travels, leaps into Africa to confront the Saracen, coupled with his incessant clanking out of books, is hardly believable. It is quite easy to forget that Ramón's life, after conversion, was guided by one overwhelming passion: the conversion of the "infidel." The Art was simply the best means to reach the desired goal. He believed that if Christian missionaries were taught the Art—he thought six months training would suffice!—the conversion of the "infidel" would be assured. He had in mind the Moslems, Jews, and Tartars, of which the first presented a clear military threat at the time. Because of the value which Lull attributed to the Art, he never tired of commending it to popes, kings, and the mendicant orders. If today it appears a rather exotic growth it should still be placed, together with Thomas Aquinas' *Summa Contra Gentiles,* at the head of those works directed to the conversion of the unbeliever. Both were inspired by the ubiquitous Raymond of Penyafort and were designed as missionary tools. They both reflect that naive rationalism which is the other side of the morbid intensity of the Middle Ages.

Although Lull sincerely believed that the world could be converted *per syllogismos Raimundi* this did not preclude him from writing several books on spirituality. They range from a sort of primer, *The Book of Clerks,* to one of the most curious works on the spiritual life, *The Book of the Lover and the Beloved (Llibre de Amic e Amat)* which is found as the fifth book of his mammoth allegorical novel, *Blanquerna*. In these works and those more directly addressed to missionary effort, the tone is not strident or bitter. Although many of the Islamic and Jewish characters depicted seem all too easily to be persuaded of the truth of Christianity, others resist conversion. In some works a final choice is not reached. On the whole, his opponents are less straw figures than most. There is far more give and take in these works than say in the early Socratic dialogues. Respect for the person of his "infidels," even affection, is reflected in the text. To explain it as merely a part of his apologetic technique would appear to be somewhat one-sided.

All of his favorite projects were failures. Even the foundation of a school at Miramar for the study of Semitic languages suffered an early demise. The Art was never given serious consideration in spite of the many works which he wrote in the wake of the *Ars Magna*. As far as we know his missionary efforts were also ephemeral. At an advanced age he converted to the crusading ideal—Clement V stirred the embers—but Christendom by now was too exhausted and disenchanted to engage in such heroic and expensive enterprises. This fierce old man oscillated between the self-pity reflected in his *Desconort* and the enthusiasm of his late works against the Averroists. Ramón Lull has been called a precursor of the computer. The Art gives him legitimate title. He might also be considered as adumbrating a sincere and rigorous dialogue between religions and cultures.

An eccentric figure vaguely reminiscent of Lull, a fellow Catalan, Mother Cardona came on the scene in the Spain of the sixteenth century, only to later withdraw in the shadow of more impressive figures. A lady in waiting who became a hermit, she emerged some years later to don the habit of the recent Discalced Carmelite Reform. Typical of the wandering holy men and women of the period—not unlike the best of the Russian *starets* of the last century—Mother Cardona aroused popular interest, no little adulation, was received at court by Philip II and befriended by Don Juan of Austria. After having been embroiled in difficulties in the Carmelite community at Pastrana, a Discalced house which did attract some strange characters, she retired to a cave neighboring the community of La Roda. Exaggerated and undisciplined, all the pathological excrescences of religious life came to the fore in her admirers. Yet, even in retrospect, some of the Carmelite Friars preferred her to Teresa of Avila. Teresa retained the fealty of the Order she founded and her Castilian sense of discipline triumphed over the wildly attractive, fanatically ascetic, spirituality of Mother Cardona.

Teresa herself was the granddaughter of a Toledan Judaizer who repented and, according to report, died a pious Christian. She was in many ways a microcosm of her age. Suffering from many successive illnesses from childhood to old age she was able to endure and transcend them. Though not immune to the religious aberrations of the day she softened and domesticated them within the boundaries of a heroic yet prudent spiritual life. Teresa is distinguished from the ecstatics and enthusiasts which proliferated in the sixteenth century by a gift for reducing the exacerbations of her rich personality to unity. This talent for organization was manifested not only in her personal but in her public life, found even within the groundswell of physical illness, psychopathology, and human contradiction. Her expertise on the governance of convents and her unusual clarity in things spiritual were paralleled by the order within disorder found in her literary works. There are repetitions, at times excessive and annoying digressions, but the thread of exposition is hardly ever lost nor the end in view compromised.

In Teresa we have a character who delights in paradox. In spite of constant pleadings of feminine weakness, Mother Teresa founded convents, wrote constitutions and kept a vigilant eye on the Carmelite Reform movement of both Sisters and Friars. A privileged sense of timing coupled with a truly superb sense of humor and an eye for human foibles made her expert in politico-religious intrigue and kept the fragile barque of the Discalced Carmelites afloat when mere human discretion would have despaired. Disclaimers of bad health, low intellectuality, wandering attention, and a veritable casebook of psychological complaints are laid to rest by her literary works of which at very least the *Way of Perfection* and the *Interior Castle (Moradas)* may be counted among the classics of the spiritual life. In many ways a highly parochial Spanish nun, ensconced rather comfortably within the framework of the *Siglo de Oro*, she was to become the most popular spiritual guide in the new world of Galileo and the mathematization of nature. Less intellectualized than many of her predecessors, Teresa added practical emphasis to the literature of mysticism. The God on the other side of the cloud of unknowing is also encountered among the pots and pans.

William James was as usual perspicacious when he suggested that there is a notion in the air that religion is probably only an anachronism, an atavistic relapse into a mode of thought which humanity has outgrown.[6] This would apply with additional force to religions' most recondite enclave, mysticism. Perhaps this is why mysticism has been allocated to psychopathology or covered by the same blanket as spiritualism, after-death phenomena, and automatic writing. This suggests that at that moment in which the human mind loses its ability to discriminate and falls into a spiritual rut in which all cows are grey, the real world of the spirit as well as the human world of culture, is lost to it.

Respect for historical complexity demands that the term "mysticism" be used in a liberal but not anarchic fashion. Pseudo-Denis and Bonaventure are highly intellectualized, logical and rigorous, asking questions, making distinctions, framing arguments. Ramón Lull is unique, closer both to pure logic and poetry. With Teresa the literature of mysticism gains in vivacity and develops full-grown within the world of Christian piety. In all four, conversion, inspiration, and aspiration to union with God are encountered. Mystical phenomena proper is suggested, perhaps even presupposed, by all, but found in detail only in the works of Teresa of Avila.

It is not the intention of the present study to pigeonhole anyone into a given slot on the ladder of Jacob. It merely proposes to give a sketch of what Christian spirituality has claimed for itself as reflected in the lives and work of these four mystical writers. If any continuity does in fact exist between the hermits of Scete, scholarly ascetics, vagabonds *a lo divino*, the monastic cloister, and mendicant theologians, it may well come to the surface and have something relevant to say to contemporary Christianity. After all, the spiritual life is ultimately reflected in the secular world; passion for God has the capacity to mold human endeavor. Its course may not be direct—detachment from created things is for the mystic always a prerequisite—but will somehow etch its character on domains far from the immediate concerns of the mystical writer. When brought to light, these submerged possibilities of Christian existence may help us find our way among the peculiar dangers provided by the ingenuity of the times. Perhaps we shall find that the only real tragedy consists in dismissing sanctity as a possibility of the human condition.

Notes

[1] *The Varieties of Religious Experience*, (New York: Modern Library, 1922), pp. 370-371.

[2] *Ibid.*, p. 265ff.; pp. 467-468.

[3] *Mysticism East and West*, (New York: Meridian, 1960), Appendix II, p. 233.

[4] The distinctions made by Irene Behn in her *Spanische Mystik* are terminologically ponderous (mystographic, mystogogic, and mystologic) but may well be useful. Cited by Baldomero Jimenez Duque, *Teologia de la Mistica*, (Madrid: BAC, 1963), p. 8, note 6.

[5] The name "Teresa of Avila" is used here although I fully agree with Father Otilio Rodriguez, OCD, that "Teresa of Jesus" holds a privileged place as it "summarizes a whole life of love and surrender to the will of Jesus." "St. Teresa of Jesus and Mental Prayer" in *Word and Spirit*, 1982, no. 4, pp. 3-13. Still, the name "Teresa of Avila" is probably more recognizable to the non-specialist and this is of great importance in a book directed to the general public.

[6] William James, *op. cit.*, p. 480.

I
Pseudo-Denis

It is a truly laborious task to investigate the origins of the speculations presented in the *Corpus Areopagiticum*[1] and the life from which it may have emerged. One is faced by a lengthy catalog of ships—philosophers, theologians, monks, hermits—which mean very little to anyone except perhaps the historical antiquarian. The hermeneutic of Theodore of Mopsuestia or the ascetical practices of Nilus are of little interest today. But the cultural and religious background of the unknown author of the *Corpus,* though a matter for conjecture, is of substantial importance to the study of Christian mysticism. The three hundred or so years which separate the Christian thinkers of Alexandria from Pseudo-Denis were charged with consequences for the development of the young and already turbulent Christian community.

A fairly accurate generalization would view the works attributed to Denis the Areopagite as comprised of two related strains. On the one hand, the intellectualist, with Plotinus on the far horizon and Proclus near at hand. On the other, a hard, basic, almost elemental strain perhaps leading back to the hermits of Scete and the monastic communities of the Thebiad. That Denis was a Syrian monk writing in the late fifth or early sixth century is usually accepted. A distinction between city and desert characterized this milieu where culture and civility confronted harsh primitiveness and rank ignorance. As long as the Christian conscience could find itself at ease—at times it was far too much at ease—in the city, it took root and flourished. But when the city was revealed as structurally hostile to Christian life some of the best men, and perhaps some of the worst, abandoned it.

They did not leave as cowards leaving the field of battle. On the contrary, they were considered athletes of God going to do battle against Satan on his preferred ground, the desert. The Rule of St. Benedict, some time later, will speak of the solitary combat of the desert. In spite of many woeful exaggerations such as those later incorporated into modern literature into, say, Anatole France's *Thais,* there is much to admire.

The Background

In spite of the temptations provided by the relatively cosmopolitan life of the cities, they became inhospitable in a more concrete manner during the Roman persecutions. Clement of Alexandria, for example, fled Egypt because of the persecution of Septimus Severus. A Christian of truly superior cultural attainments, he was convinced, adumbrating future speculation, that all knowledge serves theology. But his manner lacks the vehemence of a Peter Damian and philosophy is given a special position as the providential means by which God brought the pagan nations to Christ.[2] He improvises on the genre of *protreptikoi,* exhortations urging men to study philosophy, in his own *Protrepticus,* an invitation to conversion. Christianity is the very highest of philosophies and the *Logos* the greatest of teachers. The theme is expanded in his *Paidagogos,* in some ways an anticipation of Augustine's *De Magistro,* in which the *Logos* is seen as the pedagogue of humanity.

Philosophy has not been rendered otiose by the Christian faith. Clement emphasizes that it still serves by enabling Christians to arrive at knowledge of the content of their faith. Nevertheless, to accentuate the superiority of revelation over Greek wisdom, he has Plato composing his *Laws* in imitation of Moses and identifies the Christian ideal with that of the ideal Gnostic. But this is the *gnosis* of Christ. The *Logos* is the teacher of the world, the legislator of humanity, saviour of the human race, and founder of a new life. This "new life" begins with faith and advances towards knowledge and contemplation. Through love it reaches its final goal, deification. Clement incorporates, as part of one organic process, Christian faith, the development of its content in knowledge, love, and final beatitude.

This intertwining of philosophy and religious life where understanding is a spiritual exigency and contemplation the goal of speculation will be found in later writers, especially those influenced to some extent by Neoplatonism. Anselm comes first to mind. Insofar as his immediate influence is concerned—there is no doubt that he contributed in setting the stage for an intellectualistic mysticism such as that found in the works of Pseudo-Denis—it was probably less than that of his successors. A good case can be made that the principal influence on Pseudo-Denis was Origen, who, through the medium of Evagrius Ponticus, reached the attention of the Syrian monk.

Although a somewhat bedraggled truism, it bears repeating that Origen[3] was one of the most brilliant, erratic, inventive minds in the history of Christian thought. The later Augustine-Jerome correspondence catalogs his fall from grace. It is difficult not to sympathize even with his aberrations which are many and usually generous. The pre-existence of the soul, the final salvation of all mankind (even of Satan and his demons), and the existence of a multiplicity of worlds are not the basest of hypotheses. A life spent in controversy did not prevent him from leaving a literary production outstanding in both quality and bulk. Jerome compiled eight hundred titles and this was a rather low estimate. In any case, Origen wrote the oldest rigorous study of Christian prayer (*De Oratione*), the greatest defense of the primitive Church (*Contra Celsum*) and a superb analysis of the fundamental doctrines of Christianity (*De principiis*). Greatly influenced by Neo-platonism he still accorded a lower position to philosophy than did Clement. Many of his works became staples with the Egyptian monks and his influence is present in the very early monastic rules.

In Origen we find indications of a clear though hardly complex theory of mysticism. To begin with, in *De principiis*, he distinguishes between man as *image* and as *likeness* of God.[4] The first is the ground of perfection, the second its development which must be attained by means of human effort. It comprises the imitation of Christ and has three steps: self-knowledge, the struggle against sin, and the ascent. To begin with, the basic questions must be asked to ascertain the position of the soul vis-à-vis God. Who am I? What should I do? The struggle against sin is launched with the attack directed against its causes, viz., human passions and the "world." Asceticism joins forces with detachment to vanquish both. At this point, the ascent to spiritual perfection can take place, the soul moving from initial inner turmoil to consolations, visions, and an ever closer approximation to Christ.

Here we find, at least in outline, the later division of the spiritual life into purgative, illuminative, and unitive, albeit it is found among a welter of outlandish speculations at times. Doubtless, Origen had an exaggerated contempt for the body, almost delight in the maceration of the flesh, which goes beyond the bounds of prudent asceticism. But perhaps asceticism should not be as prudent as modernity would advise? Still, he does seem to push to an extreme the importance of celibacy as a prerequisite to the mystical quest. Perhaps the theoretical consequence of his self-castration dovetails with his notion of spirituality. In any case, such acts of self-immolation are not unique. The roughly similar case of the Islamic mystic, Ibn' Arabi, comes to mind. His magnificent defense of virginity has much to say to our rather permissive contemporary world.

It can be argued that the very intensity with which Origen presented his case was a boon to posterity. The implications of his thought were able to come to light with unusual rapidity. In spite of his deviations, Origen's contributions to what we can begin to call mystical theory were substantial. Although Clement had previously stated that spiritual perfection is likeness to God and this is attained by means of *apatheia* (indifference) and *gnosis* (knowledge of God), Origen extends, expands, and enriches this notion in his conception of the spiritual ascent to God. The resonances will reach Pseudo-Denis.

The later Alexandrian writers such as Alexander, Athanasius, and Cyril, were combatants in violent and long-lived controversies. Notions which sound unbearably exotic such as *homoousios* and *Theotokos* entered Christian belief to stay. Athanasius, with his *Life of St. Antony*[5] did much to popularize a novel way of life which was exercising an immense attraction on the men of his and later ages. It was translated into Latin by Evagrius of Antioch and its urgent call reached Augustine some years later.

Why did the life of a simple man who could neither read nor write, and like Francis of Assisi did not care for book culture, become the model of the new Christian spirituality? Aside from his remarkable longevity—did he really live 105 years?—and the plethora of miracles which were attributed to him, his dictated letters present a sane asceticism which could scarcely be considered properly mystical.[6] His personal charisma must have been exceptional given the enthusiastic response his message and subsequent legend received. He wrote letters, (somewhat grudgingly) to Emperors, fellow hermits, and monks. In his seven letters to monasteries, Antony addresses his correspondents as "sons of Israel" as only they have followed the admonition of the Lord to withdraw from the "world." Antony provided a charter for the silent life, addressed to men of all ages and temperaments, which will probably outlive the violent criticisms brought to bear against it.

Augustine may be able to shed some light on this phenomenon. After recounting how his friend Ponticianus happened to mention Antony's *Life* and his own conversion which came by way of reading it, Augustine gives an account of his own reaction. He was greatly touched and saw himself as despicable. The Latin words are trenchant: "*quam turpis...distortus et sordidus, maculosus et ulcerosus.*" The ignorant are storming heaven while Augustine and his friends fester in flesh and blood.[7] Augustine was converted but did not follow Antony to the desert.

Here we encounter a new patriotism which fuses this world and the hereafter, a flight from self and society opposed to Christ, entailing conversion from the "old" to the "new" man. What Gibbon, with his usual malice, called an "ascetic epidemic," proved to be highly contagious. Pachomius, the founder of the cenobitic life, had over seven thousand men and women living under his rule in the fourth century. A report of 394 A.D. has the dwellers in the Egyptian and Palestinian deserts about equal to the population of the towns. Scete, the Thebiad and Mount Nitria are its spiritual battlegrounds. Antony, Pachomius, Serapion, and Macarius provided the model for desert spirituality. The *Sayings of the Fathers (Apophthegmata Patrum)* became its scripture.

The desert elicited an intensity of outlook, unity of purpose, and simplicity of heart characteristic of historical end-times. When the world is perceived as old and feeble, living the last chapter of a vice-glutted existence, the effort to escape from its clutches becomes wholehearted and intense. Perhaps because of this, much found in the *Apophthegmata* strikes us as petty and crabbed, its asceticism extreme, and many of its heroes cases in psychopathology. Nonetheless, a thorough reading—and rereading—allows a kind of sweetness which permeates their preoccupations and eccentricities to be perceived, one in tone with the very urgency with which they fled from the old self and the condemned world. They were basically antisocial—though the traffic between city and desert was appreciable—very tough and very lonely. They discovered that God as well as Satan is found in the solitude of the desert. This attitude is summarized by a saying which could well have been taken directly from Plotinus:

> The abbot Allois said, "Unless a man shall say in his heart, 'I alone and God are in the world,' he shall not find quiet."[8]

The letters of Antony's successor, Ammonas, contain traces of an incipient mysticism based on the traditional notion of the long and arduous voyage of the soul to heaven. The terrible Macarius, who would provide inspiration for Jacob Arndt in the eighteenth century, comes close to full-blown mystical theory in his fifty or so Spiritual Homilies. But the emphasis remains on the ascetic ideal of the desert. The first monk to write extensively was Evagrius Ponticus, important in his own right as well as providing the bridge connecting Origen to Pseudo-Denis. In the Christian East a school of spirituality based on his speculations lasted until the fifteenth century. Yet in spite of their contributions, the desert hermits and monks were hardly a domesticated breed and, when incensed, were capable of horrifying excesses such as the murder of the pagan philosopher, Hypatia, in 405.

The Cappadocian Fathers were, in effect, ecclesiastic monks, on the whole politically sophisticated, not beyond summoning waves of monks to their aid if theological or political circumstances demanded it. Also occupied in constant disputation, Basil the Great and Gregory Nazianzen worked together and compiled the *Philokalia*, an anthology based on the works of Origen which is still read in the Eastern Church and which became an inspiration for later mystical speculation. More to the point, Gregory of Nyssa,[9] also indebted to Origen, developed a theory of the mystical life which in many ways adumbrates themes in Pseudo-Denis' *Mystical Theology* and opens new avenues of interpretation. For instance, the *Song of Songs* is considered an allegory of the love between God and the individual soul while Origen, following Jewish precedent, applied it to the love between God and his people Israel, which is to say the Christian Church. In his *Life of Moses*, Gregory adapts an approach then common in catechetical instruction in which *historia* (history) was followed by *theoria* (speculation). In the first part, he presents a summary of Moses' life and in the second proceeds to view the ascent of Moses as representing the mystical ascent of the soul to God.

In the wake of Philo, Clement, and Origen, Gregory moves allegory in the direction of mysticism. The importance of moral purification as the necessary propaedeutic to the ascent and the method of unknowing or detachment are stressed. The soul leaves behind whatever can be sensed or thought—the sensible and intelligible domains—until it reaches the invisible and incomprehensible where it "sees" God.[10] The spiritual quest is here viewed as an ascent and the need for ascetic preparation is stressed as is the importance of detachment which leads to the unknown darkness and ultimate vision. Neoplatonic influence is highly visible as it is in the *Mystical Theology*. It will take the vicissitudes of continuing speculation to mute its blatant intellectualism.

Gregory believes that man must acquire through purification what he calls "spiritual senses" which are attuned to the alien dimension of the transcendent God. Only then can he "see" God. Although those features of Moses' life which involve withdrawal from active involvement in human affairs are emphasized, a return to society takes place so that God's design may be furthered.[11] At this point Gregory is more in line with the behavior urged by Plato's analogy of the cave than with the desert ethos. In a surprising move which takes him some distance from the residual hellenistic world of Origen, Gregory replaces the traditional notion of static perfection as the goal of spiritual life by one of continual progress.[12] This will find a distant echo in John of the Cross. This progress in God becomes as infinite as is God himself.

Gregory distinguishes three stages in Moses' experience of God: a visual manifestation (light), an auditory manifestation (in the cloud), and sight within darkness. By taking some liberties with the text we can again encounter the tripartite division of the spiritual life into purgative, illuminative, and unitive stages. Gregory is the last relevant figure of Christian spirituality prior to the elusive figure of Pseudo-Denis. There are great clerics, monks, and some interesting names. We find the unfortunate Theodore of Mopsuestia, declared a heretic some 125 years after his death; Nestorius, his pupil, and the cause of much theological mischief; and the redoubtable John Chrysostom, who could agitate with equal vigor in favor of social justice and against Jews. It was also the time of Nilus who authored a work on the monastic life (*De monastica exercitatione*) but could hardly be considered a writer of mystical literature.

The Dionysian Corpus

The Neoplatonic imprint on the *Corpus Areopagiticum* is unmistakable although scholars are still debating the extent of its penetration. Whatever the final verdict there are clear echoes of Proclus, Plotinus, and Iamblichus. Over a century ago, Uberweg indicated that with Pseudo-Denis, hellenic philosophy assumes a "Christian exterior."[13] However, more recently Lossky has attempted to minimize the importance of Neoplatonic influence.[14] It still remains a matter for scholarly investigation whether the influence is direct or garnered through Christian writers such as Origen and Gregory of Nyssa. As these matters, albeit intellectually stimulating, are not directly relevant to the present theme, let us pass to the works which comprise the Dionysian *Corpus,* in particular the *Mystical Theology* and attempt to discern the main lines of its thought.[15]

Scholars have provided many intriguing hypotheses concerning the identity of the proclaimed Athenian disciple of St. Paul. Severus of Antioch, St. Basil, Ammonius Saccas, Peter the Iberian, and Dionysius, Bishop of Alexandria, have joined the medieval choice of St. Dionysius, martyr, Bishop of Paris, as the authentic Denis. Abelard's denial of the latter's candidacy caused him no little vexation from the good monks of St. Denis. The pseudonym goes back to St. Paul's discourse before the Council of the Areopagus and his reference to the "unknown God" who is "not far from any of us, since it is in him that we live, move, and exist" and the subsequent conversion of Denis the Areopagite.[16] Whoever the author of the *Corpus* is, he is prodigal in extravagant detail. He was present at the crucifixion when an eclipse of the sun occurred and also at the dormition of the Blessed Virgin Mary, was friendly with the Apostles and so on.[17] These apocryphal details served to confirm the identity of the author of these works and the disciple of St. Paul.

The leitmotif of Dionysian mysticism is the theme of the unknown God, found in its most rarified form in the *Mystical Theology* and interspersed throughout the additional three treatises and ten letters which comprise the *Corpus Areopagiticum*. They reflect a similar if not identical inspiration and present admirable coherence in both theme and structure. Because of this some scholars, among them Father Vanneste, have supported the view that the author's intention was to elaborate a vast synthesis.[18] But even if his purpose was far more modest it is clear that these works are interrelated in some way and therefore amenable to a methodological approach. Many scholars have used the *Divine Names* as the point of departure. Actually, there is no reason why the *Celestial Hierarchies* or even the letters could not be so used. In all of them themes are developed which are reflected in the *Mystical Theology*.

A word of warning before continuing. Although Denis[19] is familiar with the Scriptures—his symbolism reflects this attachment—and the content of his thought is usually orthodox even according to later standards, a reading of the *Mystical Theology* never fails to surprise. In fact, its privileged status in the literature of Christian spirituality is not immediately apparent. The reader finds the innumerable celestial beings of hellenistic mythology giving place to angels and the Neoplatonic ascent to the One transformed into elevation to the transcendent God. A faint but heady aroma of paganism remains. Perhaps the fact that of 1,702 citations made by Thomas Aquinas of the *Corpus,* only twenty refer to the *Mystical Theology*, suggests that something may be awry. Moreover, comparing this work to those of some prior Christian writers, say Gregory of Nyssa, it appears to contain at least as much residual paganism. No matter what the final verdict is, its tremendous authority and pervasive influence on future thought is unchallenged. Whether Denis should be considered a mystic proper or merely a mystical writer is a serious question which should be broached at the proper time.

Although the term "mystic(al)" was used prior to Denis, both in philosophical treatises and Christian writings, he is credited with using it normatively in its spiritual meaning. However, the term does not refer primarily to the supernatural life but rather to the secret doctrine (*mysterion*) through which man can arrive at union with a God who, though ineffable, has condescended to reveal himself through Sacred Scripture.[20] Denis speaks of two paths of ascent or "return" to God. The first is through *theology*, based on negation and realized individually. The second is through *theurgy* and takes place through the mediation of those levels of reality which are superior to man. Man ascends by incorporating into himself and into the human community those realities present on superior levels. It is in this way that the angels help man to reach out towards his transcendent goal.

As indicated, although the union of the individual soul with God— mystical union proper—is described in the *Mystical Theology*, not all aspiration to union with God is properly mystical. This latter approach is set within the framework of fourth century Neoplatonism which was, perhaps too enthusiastically, incorporated into Christian thought. *Affirmative theology* deals with the Divine Names (God's attributes) in much the same way in which your everyday believer understands them. God is powerful, wise, good, and so on. But when a higher knowledge is desired these names must be negated: God is not powerful, not wise, not good, and so forth. This is the point of departure of *negative theology*. Though the Divine Names can be used affirmatively to describe God and in this way to elevate the human soul to him, they fail to express adequately that what he is, as God, in transcending all beings, is unknowable. Even *being* can be denied to God, as he is its source and therefore superior to it.

Denis poses a radical distinction between God and creation which is reflected in human speech by those convoluted twists and turns which make talk about God possible but checkmate any attempt at accuracy. It paralyzes that all too human hubris which delights in the attempt at imprisoning God within concepts. And yet in a very real sense God is everything, beginning and end, alpha and omega. To understand this paradox of the illusive God it is necessary to approach the Dionysian notion of hierarchy, itself a good introduction to his thought. But this is a difficult enterprise because of the linear style of thinking we have inherited from modernity. Though the world is indeed full of a number of things all are more or less situated on the same level. This optic was not shared by the ancient or the medieval world. For Denis the created world is primarily a theophany, which is to say, a manifestation of the divine perfections.

It is taken for granted that the physical world in its rich and ordered variations, its multiplicity of species, present varying degrees of participation in the divine perfection. Its place on the "chain of being" determines the status of any given entity. The transcendent God is viewed as permeating the entire created universe by his presence which, like light, is diffused in all directions. Obviously, the highest beings are those closest to God, those which possess the greatest receptivity to his activity.[21] The "great chain of being" stretches from those beings closest to God to those furthest away. Denis indicates that it is possible to ascend by means of rational speculation from the visible to the invisible, from the inferior to the superior.

This conception of a vast complex structure of related but hierarchically graded levels of perfection is comprised of two principal domains, the celestial and the terrestrial. This all-embracive view held most of the Middle Ages in thrall and, strange to say, survived in a desiccated form into modernity. Note John Adams:

> Nature, which has establised in the universe a chain of being and universal order, descending from archangels to microscopic animalcules, has ordained that no two objects shall be perfectly alike, and no two creatures perfectly equal.[22]

Denis, as many Christian writers influenced by Neoplatonism, accepts a different scheme of things, a different set of priorities, than would later thinkers influenced by Aristotelianism. This view, in some ways resembling our own, is nicely if somewhat superficially reflected in the later Scholastic maxim "*nemo dat quid non habet*," nothing gives what it does not have. You cannot give away a thousand dollars unless you first have it, infect another person without first having the disease yourself, and so on. Applied to the Deity, God must exist before he creates. All well and good—and very familiar. On the contrary, in the Neoplatonic scheme, God, in order to create being, must himself be superior to being. (Denis and the Neoplatonic *Book of Causes* assertion that "being is the first of all creations," did much to stimulate metaphysical speculation in the Middle Ages and after.) In any case, in this schema, examples must be taken from other activities. The General must first outrank the Captain in order to promote him, the oak no longer an acorn so as to produce them. Though scarcely adequate these comparisons serve to prepare the way for the unfamiliar use of Nothing (No-Thing) as a privileged Divine Name. God is Nothing because he transcends being.

The Dionysian universe is truly unique, one in which an angel is, as in one of Rilke's poems, the first degree of the terrible. It resembles an El Greco canvas in which earthly matter becomes transformed into gossamer while sweeping into the realm of the sacred from which it derives its meaning. We must remember that for Denis the angelic world is neither fantasy nor is it conveniently separated from the human world. It is constituted by nine choirs, each corresponding to a different degree of divine light,[23] leading into the human world of ecclesiastical hierarchies. Every angel and man possesses a dual function: to tend towards the Good, and to communicate this good to its inferiors, in this way helping each one to ascend to his proper level.

This is to say, each angel and man is given the gift of loving God and of helping others to love him. Although the gift is, in itself, immaterial, when it is constituted on the social level it is given concrete form by means of ecclesiastical institutions and liturgical symbols. The very first chapter of the *Celestial Hierarchies* deals with the relation between the sensible and intelligible orders and the elevation from the images found in Sacred Scripture to the "supercelestial intelligences." Denis borrows the Platonic absolute/imperfect copy relation, between the real world and the physical world, while adding a Christian version of recollection. Understood in this way, his conception becomes speculatively reputable, even attractive. The "absolute ideas," perceived through their imperfect copies, exercise a power of attraction which draws the human soul up to their level.

The primary goal of hierarchy is the greatest assimilation to, and union with, God.[24] But this upward march must be aided by moral and spiritual purification. The human soul, in ascending, must endeavor to shed all traces of unlikeness to God. But this is not yet properly mystical. As Denis indicates, this is *philosophy*. Philosophers, in his seventh letter, are those who elevate themselves to God through the knowledge of things. The *mystical way* is different. It takes place through *unknowing* and dispenses with intermediaries. It follows that the universe comprised of hierarchies must be denied or bracketed. This mystical way leads to the *henosis* (union) of the *Mystical Theology*.

Denis' philosophical approach to God in some ways resembles the later approach of Rational Theology. It is decidedly not philosophical in a post-Cartesian sense but is ensconced within a cognitive process still pullulating with the life of soul, a "knowing" which incorporates both assimilation and purification. The notion that knowledge sits in the human mind as in an inert receptacle and is therapeutically neutral is basically a modern invention. In the tradition of philosophy a close analogy to Denis' view would be the ascent to the Idea-of-the-Beautiful described by Diotema in Plato's *Symposium*.[25] But the latter, in spite of its frankly religious tone, is scarcely a mystical ascent in the Christian sense.

Mystical Theology

The language of the *Mystical Theology* is really not compatible with contemporary taste. It is far too exotic—the language of the pagan mysteries with biblical resonances. It delights in lengthy phrases, opulence, and fustian. The first paragraph, a prayer to the Trinity asking for guidance, exemplifies this trend. In spite of this, the principal stages of the mystical quest are given in Denis' advice to "dear Timothy": 1) detachment from the sensible and intelligible domains; 2) the ascent through unknowing, and 3) union with God. Only through negation of self and all things will the soul ascend to the radiance of Divine Darkness.[26] He proceeds to describe the mystical journey by means of comparison with Moses' ascent on Sinai, in this respect emulating Gregory of Nyssa. The "blessed Moses" was commanded to purify himself and then to separate himself from the unpurified. After this, Moses witnessed a pyrotechnic display of trumpets and lights before ascending together with the chosen priests to the summit of the mountain and "seeing" the place where God dwells.[27] In other words, purification is followed by detachment and this by vision.

Although it would be comfortable to view the above from the vantage point of the purgative, illuminative, and unitive model, mentioned previously, which later became normative, it should first of all be understood on its own grounds. The first stage entails detachment from sense and intellect, viz., withdrawal from the mode of knowledge which is natural to man. This detachment (*aphairesis*) is not in the least haphazard but requires a methodical effort which should lead to unknowing (*agnosia*) and from this point advance to union (*henosis*) with God. These three terms, detachment, unknowing, and union, in effect synthesize Dionysian mystical speculation.

This enterprise can only be undertaken by those who possess the proper disposition: those who have been purified. In the language of the pagan mysteries Denis speaks of the "uninitiated," referring to those souls which are so enmeshed within the web of purely human categories that they are unable to envision any reality lying beyond them as well as to those whose notion of God is derived from the material world.[28] These are fundamentally intellectual defects. Why are moral, spiritual, even physical defects left unmentioned? We are not told why. Still, under a Neoplatonic dispensation they are probably included under the higher, intellectual aspect of man. In any case, the ascent is described in intellectualist terms and represented symbolically by the Moses narrative. After this initiation the path towards union with God begins to take shape.

Denis places great stress on the notion of a transcendent and unknown God. As indicated previously, a pedestrian notion of God is an ever-present temptation characteristic of the "uninitiated." In effect, God is super-essentially exhalted, totally transcendent, beyond all. Because of this, mystical revelation is experienced only by those who have passed "beyond oppositions," even those of good and evil. This is not meant in the Nietzschian sense—it is not a transvaluation of morals, but comprises a transcending of those categories which hold on the created level so as to rise even higher than the highest level of "holy beings," in other words, the celestial hierarchies. Leaving "divine light" and "sound" behind the soul plunges into the darkness where the God who is beyond all lives.[29] This must be truly frightening. Once the structures of created being have been left behind the human soul is left with nothing to hold on to. Yet it is within this void that God makes himself known.

God cannot be known through the natural operations of man as they are proportionate to created being. It follows that these operations of sensation, imagination, and cognition must be negated—bracketed— to clear the way for divine activity. The importance of *catharsis* and *apatheia*, purification of the affects and serenity, in the Eastern Patristic tradition has previously been noted. In Denis there is a slight change of emphasis which now rests on the surpassing of sensation and intellectual knowledge. He seems to be primarily concerned with an asceticism of knowing as a complement to moral asceticism, the necessary precondition to mystical union. Presupposed here is the view that the highest realities which can be perceived through sensation or thought are at best symbols for those high realities or basic ideas found immediately below God himself. On the practical level it means that sensation and thought are not the means for reaching God.

This asceticism of knowing is directed towards a complete detachment from the natural modes of human knowing as well as from their proper objects. Through it the mystic pilgrim is able to plunge into the Darkness of Unknowing where these structures are not extant. In this way the highest function of man is liberated so as to be united with the unknown and unknowable God. The human desire for activity, for appropriation, is in this way muted and the receptive capacities, of which he is so little aware, are disposed for the divine presence. Denis embraces the paradox that only by knowing nothing can that which surpasses knowledge be known.

The second chapter of the *Mystical Theology*, dense and convoluted, expands this theme. This exceptional "knowledge" of God which is derived through detachment elicits a lyrical response. It evokes praise by means of hymns and poetry, a response which will become traditional in Christian mystical literature, perhaps reaching its zenith in the lyrical effusions of John of the Cross. Denis does not in fact state that he has personally experienced mystical knowledge but merely that he desires to do so. Obviously, there is no language to describe such an experience except through song and poetry, what Thomas Aquinas once referred to as the leap of the mind breaking into sound.

The notion that the journey to God is comprised by a process of detachment is very suggestive if only because of the rather lengthy history of the term *aphairesis*. It was used by Aristotle, Plotinus, Gregory of Nyssa, and Proclus and may be translated as abstraction, divestment, withdrawal, subtraction, as in arithmetic, as well as detachment. This process which, in Denis' view, is methodical and involves withdrawal from all creaturely structures, is compared to the sculptor who removes all the excess matter in the marble he is working on and brings to light the beauty hidden within. Very much in the Neoplatonic tradition, Denis is here following Plotinus, who advised:

> Withdraw into yourself and look. If you do not find yourself beautiful yet, act as does the creator of a statue that is to be made beautiful: he cuts away here, he smooths there, he makes this line lighter, this other purer, until a lovely face has grown upon his work. So do you also.[30]

After Plotinus, Gregory of Nyssa used a modified—shall we say Christianized—version of the analogy. The very rules of sculpture are established by the Holy Spirit and the "lovely face" into which the soul is to be sculpted is Christ himself.[31] In both Plotinus and Gregory the goal of the process is to attain conformity to an objective norm by means of asceticism. Denis is advocating a total renunciation of self and world to allow that which is neither self nor world to manifest Himself. In either case, the example of the sculptor working on marble, removing those portions which hide the true beauty of the sculpture, potentially in the marble prior to sculpting, is very much to the point.

As previously stated, Denis clearly distinguishes between this negative method of detachment (or negation) from the positive method of affirmation. The latter is a descending movement which is described in terms of the past, beginning with the universal and descending to particulars, viewing God in all things from highest to lowest. As used by Denis in *The Divine Names* it follows the very order of creation. On the other hand, the method of negation mounts upward on the great chain of being moving from particular to universal, denying the applicability of all attributes to God. This movement begins with the things of the sensible world, passes on to the realities of the intelligible world, and ends in total detachment. The goal of this process is the contemplation of the Superessential Darkness, hidden by the light of existing things.

The enterprise doubtless has pagan intimations. It is similar to the Neoplatonic ascent which divests the soul of matter and enables it to move to the higher regions. Both Plotinus[32] and Proclus[33] have left impressive examples of this ascent through negations. Although Christian ascents are distinguished from these by their emphasis on love, it must be admitted that, in spite of the superb treatment given love (*eros-agape*) in the *Divine Names*,[34] it is barely alluded to by Denis in the *Mystical Theology*. Again, the Plotinian One is hardly the Christian Trinity who transcends the antinomy between one and many and is completely unknowable.

But perhaps the role of love is presupposed in the *Mystical Theology*. Denis states elsewhere that theologians call God love or charity, *eros kai agape*, as he is a force who elevates everything to himself. Moreover, God is ecstatic towards his creation, manifesting his love by dwelling in all things while remaining in himself.[35] This is a startling expression but does not allay the impression that his ascent has a marked intellectualist emphasis and seems to be in some ways closer to Plotinus and Proclus than to St. Paul.

Denis further clarifies the distinction between positive and negative theology. He lists those works in which affirmative theology is used: *Theological Outlines, Divine Names,* and *Symbolical Theology*. All of these works, except the *Divine Names*, have been lost, although the tenth letter refers to the themes discussed in the *Symbolical Theology*. All three are said to deal with specifically Christian topics centering around the two great mysteries of revelation: Incarnation, and Trinity. All three deal with words, as indicated by Denis: the *Theological Outlines* with the principal affirmations concerning God, Trinity, and the superessential Jesus, viz., the Jesus who antedates creation, the *Divine Names* with the principal names of God (Good, Being, Life, Power, et al), and the *Symbolical Theology* with the metaphorical names of God.[36] This is to say, three levels of investigation are presented: the Christian mystery proper, the intelligible names, and the sensible names. The *Mystical Theology* inverts this order as it begins with the sensible names and ends in the Christian mystery proper. While the descending order is equivalent to the structure of the created universe, the ascending motion—the way of negative theology—inverts the order and becomes an enterprise to be launched.

Each theology has its proper movement. Affirmative theology descends from the highest to the lowest and the number of conceptions—thinkables—increases progressively. Negative theology ascends from the lowest to the highest with the number of conceptions progressively diminishing until the mystic becomes silent, "voiceless" both in speech and thought, and at last united to the Ineffable. No voice, no word, no thought, is found at the summit.

Denis provides a good example of the functions of the two theologies:

> For is it not more true to affirm that God is Life and Goodness than that He is air or stone; and must we not deny to Him more emphatically the attributes of drunkenness and wrath rather than the applications of human speech and thought.[37]

As affirmative theology begins with the highest and moves to the lowest it is preferable to affirm a divine name of God (Life and Goodness) than a physical thing such as air and stone. As negative theology employs the opposite procedure it is preferable to deny metaphorical attributes such as drunkenness and wrath, than noetic activities (speech and thought). It becomes clear that affirmative theology must lead to spiritual frustration as the most extensive account of divine attributes only serves to generate more names, and these are constantly receding from their source. God remains on the other side of the process. Nevertheless, Denis insists that even blatantly anthropomorphic expressions have their place. Though not true in a literal sense, the biblical accounts of God's anger, grief, and so forth, have an important place in human worship. They stimulate the soul to move in the proper direction.

Insofar as negative theology is concerned it should be stressed that detachment (*aphairesis*) is more than a mere abandonment of all sensible and intellectual knowledge. It is also a logical operation which

moves by means of successive negations from things which are furthest
removed from God to those nearest to him. By so doing it provides an
antidote to the futility of the positive method in arriving at union with
God. The denial of each progressive level of the hierarchical universe
by means of detachment is meant to liberate the soul from the *world*
and its categories. But so far mystical union remains on the far
horizon. Denis has described a process which takes place within the
limits of nature. The answer is found in the two final chapters of the
Mystical Theology which continue to embroider the themes previously introduced, centering on detachment and its application to the
sensible and intelligible domains.

Denis begins by examining the sensible world, moving from corporeal properties such as shape, quantity, and quality, to other properties
of material existence such as change, corruption, division, and privation. All must be denied of God as he transcends all categories belong-
ing to the material order.[38] Intelligible properties are also considered
and their applicability to God also denied. God is not soul or intellect or
anything intelligible. The process of detachment/negation becomes
ruthless. God is not science, truth, kingship, or wisdom. He is not One,
not godhead, not goodness, not even spirit according to human understanding.[39] That Denis is following a traditional Neoplatonic schema
does not take the sting out of these negations, especially when he
arrives at those names which philosophers and theologians use to
address God. But the procedure should be familiar by now. It is meant
to confirm that the entire universe—which in the Dionysian scheme
comprises both things that are and things that are not—falls radically
short of God. As God cannot be known as he is, human language,
pressed to its limits in this impossible task, simply breaks down.

Whatever is below God—which is to say everything created—can
be affirmed or denied. God is beyond both affirmation and negation. In
this way the negative approach becomes an entitative paring away of
attributes derived from creatures to enable the soul to enter into a
domain in which its own mundane categories are no longer operative.
From this vantage point, the realities of the intelligible world as well
as those of the Christian faith must also be denied. Having arrived at
the limit of the knowable by means of this audacious enterprise, the

Mystical Theology ends. The God beyond light and darkness is also beyond detachment. The mystic is silent as total unknowing has been attained. Only ultimate union with God remains.

Denis indicates that this union will come about through ecstasy, another term borrowed from the pagan mysteries and incorporated into the vocabulary of Neoplatonism. In the *Divine Names* Denis speaks of man possessing two "senses." The first perceives the intelligible world, the second communes with realities above its own level.[40] It is this knowledge beyond intelligence—which he refers to as "unity"—that is directed to the supreme mystical experience of ecstasy. As we have seen, the mind is obliged to turn away from all things leaving even itself behind. It goes out of itself in ecstasy and is transported to God, united to the "Dazzling Rays," the Divine Face hidden within the darkness.

The theme is also found in the first and fifth letters, now accompanied by the weight of scriptural authority, especially St. Paul.[41] The *Mystical Theology* itself contains only sparse references to specific Christian beliefs. The opening prayer to the Trinity, the references to Blessed Bartholomew, and the Moses analogy are grand exceptions. There are few direct scriptural citations. With its undoubted scriptural resonances, his style, hieratic, obscure, and convoluted, appears at first sight to be as close to the ancient mysteries as to the new mysteries of the Christian Church. Denis will refer to Bishops as *mystagogoi*, priests as *photistikoi*, and deacons as *kathartikoi*. The very notion of ecstatic union is originally pagan and found in Christian literature only with Ignatius of Antioch, and this in spite of analogous phenomena encountered in the Hebrew prophets and the charismatic urges of the early Church. The notion of the ascent is found in Plotinus and Proclus, the most perfect blessedness is contact with the One. According to Plotinus' disciple, Porphyry, the master enjoyed this experience four times during the period of six years in which they were closely associated.

Nonetheless, the ascent described in the *Mystical Theology*, precisely because of its incorporation within Christian belief, is substantially different from that of the pagan Neoplatonists. Denis opposed contemporary Neoplatonism on many major issues. It should suffice to mention his views on matter (more optimistic), on the pre-existence and transmigration of souls (outright denial), and the negative evaluation of the body (it also is a member of Christ). Furthermore, his fusion of *eros* and *agape* was probably meant to discourage pagan enthusiasm, and the absolute supremacy of the Trinitarian God precludes conflation with the Plotinian One. In addition, the negative element which the ascent is meant to transcend is not multiplicity per se as it is with Plotinus. For Denis it is the world and its structures which stand in the way of the soul's ultimate fruition.

The Neoplatonic strain, though very much in evidence, is incorporated into a different universe of discourse. Denis did not enjoy the luxury of choosing from a multiplicity of philosophic idioms to express his Christian faith. Neoplatonism held a unique position in early Christianity and presented both practical advantages and a vision of things not unlike that of the believing community. In spite of the many dangers which were doubtless involved, Neoplatonism presented Christianity with a highly developed, finely honed instrument for the understanding, development, and defense of the faith.[42]

The *Mystical Theology*, then, presents a method of renunciation or detachment which leads to unknowing. It takes for granted the Neoplatonic world-view and reverses the order of emanation-creation, ascending from the lower to the higher orders of reality. It terminates with the denial of all language regarding God. By means of this denial, the soul enters unknowing and faces the Divine Darkness. The last stage, union with God, must remain undescribable. The soul is left in darkness to vault into another domain where the categories of the created universe no longer hold. This experience cannot be expressed in language. What happens beyond, happens beyond. No more can be said.

Epilogue

It was not the paradoxical Denis, straddling both Christianity and Neoplatonism, who exercised a pervasive fascination on the future. It was Denis, the disciple of St. Paul. The *Corpus Areopagiticum* was first cited in a dispute between Orthodox and Monophysite clergy in 533, and, ironically, rejected by the Orthodox representative, Hypatius of Ephesus, as apocryphal. But they soon gained acceptance in the East due to the authority of Maximus the Confessor. They were later accepted in the West by Pope St. Gregory and Pope St. Martin who cited them as an authority at the Lateran Synod of 649.

The translation of these works was initiated by Hilduin—a rather botched up attempt, which was continued by John Scotus Erigena at the request of Charles the Bald. The Dionysian influence permeates his spectacular *De Divisione Naturae*. His translation was followed by others in time, including those of Grosseteste, Sarracenus, and Marcelo Ficino. Perhaps because of these translations, the Dionysian imprint is found in varying degrees in otherwise dissimilar thinkers such as Abelard, Bonaventure, Albert the Great, Thomas Aquinas, Meister Eckhart, and Nicholas of Cusa.

To some extent the inspiration of the original author fell victim to the sub-apostolic authority of Denis. The translation of the *Mystical Theology* by Sarracenus accompanied by a commentary by Gallus—of great influence on later medieval thought—muted its more strident Neoplatonic tones and made it palatable to the theological temper of the day. This is reflected in the works of theologians such as Richard of St. Victor. The intellectualist, lyrical bias of Neoplatonism was harmonized with the dramatic bias of Christian belief reflected in the affective trend in spirituality originally introduced by Augustine. Denis, perhaps in spite of himself, became the father of Christian mysticism in the West.

But this resolution does not take place in the *Corpus* itself. Because of historical accident or divine providence, Denis found himself at the juncture of two contrasting forms of thought. Christianity represents the *dramatic* type. God intervenes in history by means of unpredictable acts. The reasons which undergird these occurrences remain obscure. Neoplatonism is a *lyrical* form.[43] Its object of contemplation is the ultimate reality of things reflected in the life of the mind which contains the very structure of nature. The two styles cannot coexist without dissonances, and dissonances there are in the *Corpus Areopagiticum*. In the *Mystical Theology* it is the divine incomprehensibility which provides a brake against the danger of regression to Neoplatonic pantheism. The negative way detaches the soul from the world and in this case it is very much a Neoplatonic *mundus*. It brackets the world system and places the soul beyond its strictures.

Although the inspiration of the *Corpus* reaches into the modern world touching Spinoza, the German Idealists, and Bergson, it is in the works of John of the Cross that the sea-change it undergoes becomes most apparent.[44] His use of the Dionysian metaphor "Ray of Darkness," found in both the *Mystical Theology* and the *Celestial Hierarchies*,[45] illustrates the point. Building on the ultimate identity of night and inaccessible light (found in Denis' fifth letter), John of the Cross views the ascent of the soul to God as a journey in which night is gradually transformed into light, having its inception at *prima noche* and its goal at the *despendiente*. Throughout the journey flame is both the cause and the goal of night.

He refers to the Ray of Darkness metaphor in several passages, heavy with scriptural citations, which at times are accompanied by texts from Aristotle. The Ray of Darkness is identified with mystical theology, the highest knowledge of God which is received in a supernatural manner and "secret" even to the mind that receives it.[46] Aristotle is used to buttress St. Paul's statement that there is no proximate means among created things by which the soul can be united to God. Faith is the sole "ladder" leading to God as everything else is disproportionate to the divine reality.[47] In identifying Mystical Theology and the Ray of Darkness, John is disengaging mysticism from a primarily abstract and speculative level, to place it within a practical, psychological, and religious context. Aristotle is used to lend support to John's contention that when an incompletely purified soul is given contemplation, natural reason, *el acto de su inteligencia natural* is darkened to some degree.[48]

John uses the Dionysian nocturnal images clustering around the Divine Darkness to depict the terrors of the unpurified soul as it approaches God. Infused contemplation is able to produce intense suffering. The "nights" of sense and spirit provide the required purification which is the propaedeutic to union with God. Here again the theoretical is transformed into the practical as the process of detachment—in Denis primarily a noetic task dealing with negations—becomes an ascetic process grounded on self-negation.

Strange to say, the Thomistic-Aristotelian amalgam which John was taught at Salamanca does not cohere any more satisfactorily with his spirituality than did Denis' Neoplatonism. In the *Cantico,* John faults both the paucity of knowledge man has of God and the imperfections which accompany union on contemplation as Ray of Darkness. This is to say, the mystic enjoys only an imperfect image of the fruition of the blessed in the after-life. Nevertheless, this is the most which can be experienced as it is the most the human soul, given its intrinsic limitations, can endure.[49] But it is still like a "faint whisper" from the Beloved.

But if, as Thomas Aquinas teaches, understanding must precede love, the critical question arises: how is infused contemplation possible? John answers that, although contemplative knowledge is like a Ray of Darkness to the understanding (obscure and confused), yet God communicates both knowledge and love in one single act.[50] But mystical knowledge, unlike natural knowledge which is clear and distinct, is general and obscure. It seems that at this point the workings of grace in the human soul have replaced Denis' "unity" which enjoys communion with the transcendent domain. Moreover, love is explicitly introduced as forming the very core of the ascent.

Denis' rationalism has suffered a substantial modification. The Neoplatonic language of participation and the emphasis on transcendent beauty is absent. Also, while Denis indicates that the soul enters into darkness *after* purification, John believes that the process of purification is itself darkness. Unlike Denis' God who surpasses being, John's God surpasses only the creaturely mode of being. Moreover, although for Denis ecstatic contemplation is a suprarational state its relation to the method of negations remains somewhat hazy. We may ask, in the language of a later era, is it natural or supernatural? There is no question as to the position of John of the Cross. It is reflected in his insistence on the passive nature of infused contemplation.

Nonetheless, the resemblances between the two are profound and demonstrate a continuity of inspiration and, in some cases, even of content. In both we find an overpowering awareness of God's transcendence, certitude that man is called to participate in divinity but that from his place in the created world the call is heard but faintly. There is also agreement on the need for ascetic purification to dispose the soul for its ascent, in both a sense of urgency fueled by awe in the presence of God. The metaphor enjoys a privileged status. Denis states that theology uses poetry since it provides a naturally efficacious means of access to the human mind,[51] and John insists on the power of poetry to express that which lies beyond mere words.[52]

John of the Cross is closer to the contemporary world chronologically than is Denis though perhaps no less alien to it. If a Dionysian world, structured into varying degrees of theophanic manifestation, is difficult to comprehend, so also is the path of *nadas*. Although the anonymity of the author of the Dionysian *Corpus* and the vague outlines of his world add to other difficulties of interpretation, the historical clarity of the sixteenth century Spanish world, scarcely appreciated today, generates its own difficulties. That in spite of all vicissitudes a certain though tenuous continuity exists between Denis, John, and ourselves is a tribute to the staying power of spiritual inspiration and the highest aspirations of mankind.

The goal of the Dionysian writings is the greatest possible assimilation to, and union with, God. If time has obscured the speculative content and blunted its language, if the poetry rings harshly, this does not really detract from the power of Denis' vision or the beauty of his quest. In a world such as ours, his splendid vision of a multileveled and multicolored universe proclaiming the glory of God in voices of varying timbre, might well be a shape in chaos. The journey of the soul, detaching itself progressively from all things, ascending to unknowing and union with God, was incorporated into the mainstream of Christian spirituality. It has not been an unprofitable servant.

Notes

[1]The *Corpus Areopagiticum* is comprised of four treatises and ten letters. They are *De divinis nominibus, De Mystica Theologia, De Caelesti hierarchia* and *De ecclesiastica hierarchia*. The Greek text is found in Migne, PG, v. III, (Paris, 1889). The *Mystical Theology* in cols. 997-1064. The *Corpus* has been

translated by Maurice de Gandillac, *Oeuvres Complètes du Pseudo-Denys L'Aréopagite,* (Paris: Aubier, 1943), which includes useful indices. A bilingual (Greek/French) edition of the *Mystical Theology* and letters I and V is given by J. Nanneste, S.J., *Le Mystère de Dieu,* (Bruges: Desclée de Brouwer, 1959) pp. 225-245. English translations of the *Mystical Theology* include C. E. Rolt, *Dionysius the Areopagite on the Divine Names and the Mystical Theology,* (London: SPCK, 1957), and *The Mystical Theology and the Celestial Hierarchies of Dionysius the Areopagite,* (Surrey: The Shrine of Wisdom, 1949).

[2]Refer to *The Writings of Clement of Alexandria,* trans. W. Wilson, (Edinburgh: T & T Clark, 1872). For the relation between faith and knowledge see *Stromata,* II, 6; VI, 7, 18; VII, 10.

[3]Refer to Jean Daniélou, *Origène,* (Paris: A. Fayard, 1948).

[4]*De principiis,* 3, 6, 1.

[5]A good summary introduction to the literature of the desert is given by Helen Waddell, *The Desert Fathers,* (Ann Arbor: The Univ. of Michigan Press, 1957).

[6]Johannes Quasten, *Patrologia,* trans. I. Oñatibia, (Madrid: BAC, 1962), II, p. 157.

[7]*Confessions,* VIII, 6, 15; 7, 17; 8, 19.

[8]*Sayings,* XI, v. Waddell, *op. cit.,* p. 108.

[9]A readable introduction to the thought of Gregory is an anthology selected and with an introduction by Jean Daniélou, *From Glory to Glory: Texts from Gregory of Nyssa's Mystical Writings,* trans. H. Musurillo, (New York: Scribner, 1961). Also recommended is Jean Daniélou, *Platonisme et Théologie Mystique,* (Paris: Aubier, 1944).

[10]*Life of Moses,* trans., intro., & notes by A. J. Malherbe and E. Ferguson, (New York: Paulist Press, 1978), II, No. 162 [pg. 95].

[11]*Ibid.,* II, No. 18 [p. 59]; I, No. 56 [p. 46]; II, No. 55 [pgs. 66-67].

[12]*Ibid.,* p. 148, note 84.

[13]Friedrich Ueberweg, *History of Philosophy,* trans. George S. Morris, (New York: Scribner, 1871), I, p. 259.

[14]Vladimir Lossky, *The Mystical Theology of the Eastern Church,* trans. by the Fellowship of St. Alban & St. Sergius, (Cambridge: James Clarke & Co. Ltd., 1968), p. 29ff.

[15]Among the better works on Denis are Jean Vanneste, *op. cit.,* René Roques, *L'Universe dionysien: Structure hiérarchique du monde selon le pseudo-Denis,* (Paris: Aubier, 1954), and Endre von Ivánka, *Hellenisches und Christ-liches im Fruebyzantinischen Geistesleben,* (Vienna: Herder, 1948).

[16]Acts 17:16-34.

[17]*De Div. Nom.,* III, 2.

[18]Vanneste, *op. cit.,* p. 15ff.

[19]To avoid confusion from this point on we shall refer to the author of the *Corpus Areopagiticum* as Denis.

[20]*De: Div. Nom.,* I, 1.

[21]*Ibid.,* V. 6; V. 5.

[22]Cited by Russell Kirk in *The Conservative Mind,* (South Bend: Gateway, 1978), p. 85.

[23]*De Cael. hier.,* VI, 2.

[24]*Ibid.,* III, 2.

[25]*Symposium,* 209e-212c.

[26]*Myst. Theol.,* I, 1.

[27]*Ibid.,* I, 3.

[28]*Ibid.,* I, 2.

[29]*Ibid.,* I, 2-3.

[30]*Enneads* I, 6, 9. The Mackenna translation: *Plotinus: The Enneads,* (London: Faber and Faber Ltd., 1956).

[31]*Tractatus prior in psalmorum inscriptiones,* xi.

[32]*Enneads,* V, 9, 3-4.

[33]*Elements of Theology,* trans. and notes by E. R. Dodds, (Oxford: The Clarendon Press, 1933), prop. 209, p. 183. Also refer to Henri-Dominique Saffrey, "New Objective Links Between the Pseudo-Dionysius and Proclus" in *Neoplatonism and Christian Thought,* ed. by Dominic J. O'Meara, (Norfolk: Int. Society for Neoplatonic Studies, 1982), pp. 64-74.

[34]*De. Div. Nom.,* 4, 12-18; 2, 10.

[35]*Ibid.* 4, 13.

[36]*Myst. Theol.,* 3.

[37]*Idem.*

[38]*Ibid.,* 4.

[39]*Ibid.,* 5.

[40]*De Div. Nom.,* 7, 1.

[41]Rom. 11:32; 2 Cor. 9:5; Phil. 4:7.

[42]For a brief recent statement see John N. Findlay, "Why Christians Should be Platonists" in *Neoplatonism and Christian Thought,* pp. 223-231.

[43]The distinction between the dramatic and the lyrical is taken from Emile Bréier, "Sur le Problème Fondamental de la Philosophie de Plotin." *Etudes de Philosophie Antique,* (Paris: PUF, 1955), p. 219ff.

[44]Refer to *Vida y Obras Completas de San Juan de la Cruz,* introductory study by Fr. Crisógono de Jesús, (Madrid: BAC, 1960). Perhaps the most

perceptive study of his mystical theory is given by Fr. Federico Ruiz Salvador, Introducción a San Juan de la Cruz, (Madrid: BAC, 1968). A much lengthier and more ambitious work is Georges Morel, *Le Sense de L'Existence selon S. Jean de la Croix*, 3 vols., (Paris: Aubier, 1960-1).

[45] *Myst. Theol.*, 1, 1; *De Cael. hier.*, 9, 3; 15, 8.

[46] *Subida*, II, 8, 6.

[47] *Ibid.*, II, 8, 5.

[48] *Noche*, II, 5, 3.

[49] *Cantico*, XIV, 16.

[50] *Llama*, III, 49.

[51] *De Cael. hier.*, 2, 1-2.

[52] *Cantico*, Prol., nos. 1-2.

II
Bonaventure

There are some periods of history which are times of incubation, in which problems and trends of later generations begin to take shape. The twelfth century was one of these periods. It exercised an uncommon attraction on historians and aesthetes alike. A revolutionary spirit was afoot, a nostalgia for paradise which made the aspiration for the descent of the Heavenly Jerusalem even more urgent. It took many radical forms, one of which is illustrated by Arnold of Brescia's checkered career. His opposition to clergy and Pope, his rejection of the sacraments and priesthood, adumbrates the more explosive movements of the late Middle Ages and modernity.

In his own day, Arnold was emulated in theory, practice, and instinct. Hugo Speroni, for example, preached a dessicated spirituality which rejected the rites of the Church as idolatrous inventions. Peter Waldo's "Poor Men of Lyon" embraced the cause of poverty with such singleminded tenaciousness that they eventually separated from the established Church. Amaury of Bêne professed a nebulous pantheism and the divinity of man while Peter de Bruys, more pragmatic, advocated direct action: the suppression of traditional worship and the burning of churches. Perhaps most exotic were the Cathars who took man's aspiration for purity to its radical if bizarre conclusion. They were scarcely Christian, rejected the sacraments, the priesthood, and that aggregate of symbols, traditions, and rituals which comprised Christendom.[1]

The spiritual temper of the times which led to this revolutionary euphoria was paralleled by changes within the Church itself. Devotion to the humanity of Christ comes into its own. Increased devotion to the Blessed Sacrament, perhaps a reaction against the depredations of Catharism, is reflected in the introduction of the elevation of the host. The mystery plays, liturgical and miracle dramas, sculpture and architecture, all tender devotion to the person of Christ. The cult of the

Virgin Mary also burgeons. It will reach a new height with the construction of the magnificent Gothic cathedrals of the following century and is reflected in the *Salve Regina*. An increased sensitivity to aesthetic beauty is found together with a fresh awareness of the material world. Allegorical interpretation begins to lose its pre-eminence.[2] There seems to be a humanizing of devotion along with a diminution in the awareness—so dreadfully vivid to their immediate predecessors—of the realities of the afterlife.

Catharism may well have been a reaction against this trend. Its origins can be traced back to the Christian Gnostic speculations of Valentinian and Basilides. Their immediate precursors were the Bogomils, an obscure sect, whose teachings were introduced into Europe by the merchant class. They went so far as to establish "bishoprics," settling in the area between the Rhine and the Pyrenees. The second See which they established, at Albi in southern France, provided them with the name by which they are usually identified, the *Albigensians*. Their doctrine seems to have been a rather unsophisticated rehashing of ancient Gnostic speculations. They professed a rank dichotomy between spirit and matter, antipathy if not hatred for the physical world, a belief in the malevolent nature of the Creator and consequent rejection of the greater part of the Hebrew Scriptures. Only thirteen prophets, the five books of Solomon, and the Psalms, were received into the Cathar canon.[3] Jesus Christ was considered to be the "messenger" sent by the transcendent "good God" to counter the designs of the evil Creator. After Jesus' death, Satan brought the Church into existence. Hovering in back of this melange lies the ancient Gnostic hatred for life and the hubris which begs to be saved from matter in all of its manifestations. Although attracting men from all ranks it had a special appeal to women, scriveners, artisans, and weavers.

It is surprising that Christianity was threatened several times within the period of a millennium by variations of this heretical grotesque. The current outbreak, the Albigensian, was finally suppressed by a violent, bloody, twenty year crusade (1208-1229), and prior to this they had drawn fire from the ever-vigilant Bernard of Clairvaux. The Albigensian remnant either went underground or fled from Provence to Italy and Catalonia where their influence could be perceived for centuries. The ghost of Catharism still haunts the Christian world.

A Cathar Council was held at Toulouse as early as 1167. At approximately the same time, the new world of "courtly love" was being formed around the striking figure of Eleanor of Aquitaine. The influence of Catharism may have reached the Master of the *roman courtois* himself. His romances evidence an apologetical turn probably aimed at the formation of a different type of mankind.[4] From an orthodox viewpoint its principal tenets were distasteful and suspect. The salvation of man through woman with the eternal feminine replacing the Church has an air of blasphemy about it. Perhaps the spiritualization of the carnal found in much of French literature finds its origins here. In any case, the *gai savoir* was probably not without its links to Catharism.

In spite of the mass attraction exercised by Catharism and courtly love there is something epicene and sickly about them and it is doubtful whether either could have been successfully grafted on to Christian stock. The movement which did in fact threaten to destroy the Church and fragment society emerged from medieval variations on the theology of history following in the wake of Augustine's *City of God*. Contrary to the majority trend of medieval historiography which believed that the world was decomposing by a sort of inverse evolution—Gerloh von Reichersberg, Otto von Freising, and Hildegard von Bingen represent this view—other thinkers were frankly optimistic. Hugo of St. Victor envisioned a slow but sure advance of the Kingdom of Christ and Anselm of Havelberg interpreted history as a lengthy process of education under the direction of the Divine Pedagogue.

The apogee of this melioristic view of history was reached in the works of Abbot Joachim of Fiore,[5] "*il calabrese abate Giovacchino di spirito profetico dotato*" who, through his interpretation of scripture, developed a novel Christian vision of history and provided the point of departure for the elaboration of the "Eternal Gospel." He divided the history of the world into three periods each corresponding to a Person of the Trinity. The era of the Father extended from creation to the

Incarnation, that of the Son from the Incarnation to the thirteenth century, and that of the Holy Spirit from this to the end-times. Each era involves a different relationship between God and man and consequently different relations among men themselves. Reason is followed by wisdom, and wisdom by the plenitude of intelligence. Servanthood gives way to filial submission which in turn will give way to liberty. Discipline is followed by activity which will be ultimately crowned by contemplation.[6]

This coming era will be brought into existence by the direct intervention of the Holy Spirit. Revolutionary changes will occur. A new religious order will preach throughout the world and effect mass conversions. The hierarchical Church will be destroyed and replaced by a universal community of contemplatives. Here is the theological basis for the transmutation of the Medieval Order, a spiritual and social alchemy. Joachim died in 1202 and although his speculations on the Trinity were condemned by the Fourth Lateran Council in 1215, it did not appear at the time that he had provided the theoretical groundwork for the most explosive of medieval ideologies.

Today we look at the strange, hieratic configurations of the Joachimite *Liber Figurarum* in astonishment. The circles, columns, trees with intertwining branches, flowers, demons, and angels mean very little to us. They meant much more to the medieval Christian. An underground of sorts was established which disseminated Joachim's works—something in the line of the fairly recent Teilhard phenomenon—to an increasingly curious and fascinated audience. When the abbot of the order founded by Joachim was obliged to take refuge in the Franciscan convent of Pisa, he brought with him several of his writings. In 1254, Gerard of Borgo San Donnino, a Franciscan who had lived in Pisa, published his *Introduction to the Eternal Gospel,* an edition of Joachim's three major works[7] with an introduction and glosses. In this work the Franciscan Order is identified as the privileged community destined to bring about the desired metamorphosis in society and St. Francis is viewed as inaugurating this new age of the Holy Spirit.

This vision found a favorable reception by many Franciscans, especially among the most fervent and fanatical of the brethren—the Spirituals or *Zelanti*—who believed that the spirit of St. Francis had been betrayed by Elias and his successors. The most radical of these Spirituals—as opposed to the Conventuals—would continue a phantom existence within the Order even after the proceedings against their leader, John of Parma. The struggle was vicious, the victory of the Conventuals pyrrhic, and this permanently troubled and restless element joined with the detritus of other sects to form a sort of counter-church which remained the breeding ground of rebellion and heresy for over the next few centuries.

Background

At the very center of these disputes was Bonaventure (Giovanni di Fidanza),[8] Minister General of the Friars Minor for eighteen years, the successor to John of Parma whom he was obliged to prosecute. Although there is some confusion regarding the exact date of the investigation—they range from 1257 to 1263—the most convincing arguments favor a late date.[9] This would indicate that Bonaventure did not act immediately against John of Parma but was obliged to because of the urgency of the case. By this time Gerard of Borgo San Donnino's *Introductorius* had been condemned by Pope Alexander IV and Gerard himself closeted incommunicado in a Franciscan convent. The process against John of Parma, a man of reputed sanctity, was certainly a difficult and unrewarding task.

Salimbene, the historian, makes no secret of John's Joachimistic leanings.[10] It seems that his defense and professions of faith at the inquest were evasive and were not accepted by Bonaventure. But John was not condemned as the influential Cardinal Ottoboni-Freschi intervened in his favor and the inquest ended rather abruptly with a show of amity. After the ordeal, John requested and obtained permission to retire to the hermitage of Greccio. Later, he retired to Francis' Mount Alverna where he breathed his last in the odor of sanctity.

It is one of the ironies of history that whatever the magnitude of his contributions to the Church, the Franciscan Order, speculation, and spirituality, Bonaventure has been unable to live down his role as the persecutor of John of Parma and the *Zelanti*. The historian of the Spirituals, Angel Clareno, with understandable bitterness, accuses Bonaventure of duplicity, iniquity, and violence.[11] The *Historia Sep-*

tem Tribulationem Ordinis Minorum is an acid indictment of Bonaventure and the Conventuals as well as a moving tribute to the suffering and frustrated aspirations of the Spirituals. To be sure, there was reason enough for disaffection. Francis' Rule had suffered modification, the early Lives of the saint were withdrawn and replaced by Bonaventure's own work, worse still, learning and property were on the rise. They must have felt that Satan was looming threateningly. In spite of this, even Angel Clareno recognized Bonaventure's personal sanctity[12] and the times were such that a good case could be made that the very survival of the Order and the tranquility of .the Church depended on immediate, drastic, perhaps harsh measures.

Bonaventure was a prolific controversialist. His *Collationes de decem praeceptis* and the later *Collationes in Hexaemeron* were directed against the followers of Siger of Brabante who were attempting to win over the University of Paris to Aristotelian naturalism and rationalism. On a different front the *Apologia Pauperum* was launched against the secular clergy who had impugned the mendicant ideal of poverty, a polemic in which Thomas Aquinas and John Peckham also intervened. He was credited with great preaching talents as well as exceptional diplomatic skills. The election of Gregory X to the Papacy and the reunion of the Greek Church with Rome were, at least in part, due to his efforts. He was chary of accepting honors, rejecting the Archbishopric of York. However, he did accept the Cardinalate under the title of Cardinal-Archbishop of Albano. Bonaventure died on July 15, 1274, at the convent of Friars Minor at Lyon.

We have indicated that Angel Clareno believed that Bonaventure bears the responsibility for silencing the best elements within the Franciscan Order and betraying the spirit of St. Francis. A contemporary historian faults him, together with his "master," Alexander of Hales, for the harsh measures taken by the Inquisition against the heretics of the day.[13] But a less negative opinion can be accepted without undue partisanship. If one considers Bonaventure's principal adversaries, Joachimism and Latin Averroism, it seems that they represent the opposite poles of the same danger to Christianity. Joachimism desired to "spiritualize" the Church by disestablishing the hierarchy, eliminating signs and symbols so that the hidden spiritual realities would be revealed. The *Zelanti* in the end became small, crabbed, and scarcely believable.

The Latin Averroists desired to dispense with the supernatural order and place mankind in an exclusively natural world in which the human mind is the ultimate ground of truth. In this case, once again, the Church would be superfluous. The autonomy of reason can be every bit as dangerous to Christianity as unbridled enthusiasm; the Active Intellect every bit as explosive as the Joachimist Holy Spirit. Bonaventure seems to have done his best to defend the Christian order as he understood it from its most dangerous foes while attempting to protect his own Order from internal disruption and from external attack.

His works reflect a modified Augustinianism in spite of his extensive knowledge of Aristotle to whom he had an instinctive aversion. This knowledge is reflected much more in his terminology than in the content of his thought. He preferred Plato and Plotinus to Aristotle, and Augustine to all three. Sincerely convinced of the dangers presented by Aristotelianism he opposed it with vigor on most of the central issues of the day. The title of one of his works provides a clue to his thought: *The Reduction of all the Sciences to Theology.* The Christocentric character of his work is summarized by its conclusion, that all the sciences are directed to union with God and this takes place through love.[14] Christ himself is at the very center of the sciences. Another work, *Christus, Unus Omnium Magister,* distinguishes between knowledge through faith, knowledge through reason, and contemplation.[15] As Father Maurer suggests, "for St. Bonaventure the true purpose of philosophy is to foster devotion and to help reach a mystical union with God."[16] Faith expanded by philosophy issues into theology which itself leads to contemplation and, ultimately, to the vision of God.

In Bonaventure's thought, the abstract and defecated intellectualism of Denis is found in attenuated form. Here, philosophical speculation comprises only the first stages of the journey of the soul to God. The two "theologies" of Denis are here synthesized into two stages of one process in which the negative stage acts as the corrective for the affirmative. Bonaventure is following in the footsteps of Anselm and monastic culture; in fact his solution rather closely resembles that given by Thomas Aquinas.

However Bonaventure, true to his Franciscan heritage, stresses the importance of love in the spiritual life to a greater extent than does Anselm. Instead of breaking off, terminating the enterprise when the ultimate goal has presented itself, Bonaventure presses the quest to its completion. This impatience reflects the special status he accords to faith and love as well as his less than enthusiastic view of the powers of human reason. Though Anselm might have agreed that philosophy is the medium of access to other, higher domains, he would not have accepted Bonaventure's view that it is of little value except as a stage of a process into which it is incorporated. The Bonaventurian version of the ancient monastic *peregrinatio in stabilitate* exudes clear resonances of earlier Neoplatonic speculations. The activity of thought is not merely directed towards the formulation of solutions. It also exercises a therapeutic effect on the soul. Thinking about the highest realities— and the very highest is God—is the most efficacious form of spiritual therapy. Thought, when expanded by love, generates a motion which propels the soul towards the ultimate source of knowledge.

Bonaventure is not primarily interested in the "natural" man—a humanity in the image of Adam before the Fall—but in humanity after the Fall, historical man who is elevated by grace. But because of his existential predicament it is impossible for man to arrive at truth through mere reason. Christ must help him in this enterprise:

> . . . the truth, taking the form of Christ, has constituted himself as ladder [to God], mending the first ladder which was broken in Adam.[17]

The human soul cannot rise to contemplation of God through speculation because the philosopher, heir to the depredations of original sin, ignores the objective order of things. Bonaventure summarizes the human task in the following way: "to begin with the firmness of faith, continue through the serenity of wisdom, and reach the suavity of contemplation."[18] The movement is in line with the Augustinian tradition and reproduces the Anselmian progression of faith, understanding, contemplation, and vision.

Like Thomas Aquinas and other contemporaries, Bonaventure felt the affects of the political, religious, and speculative vicissitudes of the day. When the condemnations of 1277 attempted to curb the proliferation of theological novelty a mixed company was involved. Not only the Latin Averroists but several propositions of moderates such as Thomas Aquinas were condemned. As a representative of traditional Augustinianism, Bonaventure was not affected. His difficulties were speculative and he left certain essential problems hanging without adequate resolution. Most important, the problem of illumination, dating back to Augustine, was left hanging, like the sword of Damocles, over the heads of his followers. Had he taken a further step, the natural capacity of man to know the truth would have been denied. But this step he did not take. All the energy and acuity of Matthew of Aquasparta was insufficient to solve the problem. In other cases, wild interpretations of his thought caused no little mischief. In Peter John Olivi we encounter a utopian Bonaventurianism, its rigor corroded and its sobriety weakened through contact with the radicalism of the Franciscan Spirituals.

The Journey of the Mind to God

The Franciscan inspiration of the *Itinerarium* is evidenced at the very beginning of the work. Francis and his Seraph-vision on Mount Alverna are used as the model for the ascent of the soul to its mystical home in God while the stigmata becomes the visible sign of elevated contemplation. The created universe, comprised of the hierarchy of material and intelligible entities, provides the path by which the soul ascends to God. The journey begins in the material world, continues within the human soul and then rises above to its transcendent source. In traditional Augustinian fashion, the ascent is made by passing from the external to the internal and from the temporal to the eternal.[19]

Bonaventure states in the prologue to the work that it was composed thirty-three years after the death of St. Francis when, searching for peace of soul, he withdrew to Mount Alverna. There he arrived at the realization that Francis' vision of the Seraph in the form of the crucified Christ symbolized both the high degree of his mystical experience and the path to attain it.[20] The six wings of the Seraph allegorically represent six progressive "illuminations" which dispose the human soul to arrive at ultimate peace through the "ecstatic elevations" of Christian wisdom, *per exstaticos excessus sapientiae christianae.*[21] Each of these illuminations is comprised of two aspects. The first meditates on the reflection of God in the faculties of the soul. This is to say, that the world of nature and the world of grace complement each other in providing the steps by which the soul ascends, to contemplation.

The journey passes through three levels of created beings which are arranged according to the degree of proximity to their source. They are vestiges, images, and likenesses. A vestige is a distant though distinct representation of God; an image, a proximate and distinct representation; and likeness (*similitudo*) entails resemblance through grace. Vestiges are related to God as to their causal principle, images as objects of knowledge, and likenesses by infused gift. The natural operations of creatures pertain to the vestige category, the intellectual operations through which the soul knows truth belong to the image category, while meritorious works corresponding to grace to the likeness category.[22] If an additional observation may be added to the theme without undue fatigue perhaps the most succinct formulation of the theme given by Bonaventure is found in *De scientia Christi*: "every creature that proceeds from God is a vestige, the creature who knows God is an image, only he in whom God lives is a likeness."[23]

Bonaventure insists that the precondition to this journey is to be a *vir desideriorum*, a man of desires, citing Daniel 9:13 and Psalm 37:9. This desire is generated in two ways, through affective prayer of great intensity and through insight by which the soul is transformed into rays of light.[24] He invites the reader to experience the "groans of prayer" through Christ crucified. Speculation detached from prayer is useless. The goal of the *Itinerarium* is to glorify, praise, and "savor" God—a call which is hardly limited to philosophers and theologians.

The *Itinerarium* is divided into six chapters which correspond to the wings of the Seraph, and an additional seventh chapter, dedicated to mystical ecstasy. The note of a clearly Christian piety is immediately sounded. Although the journey is well-ordered and intellectually satisfying to an extreme, its point of departure and its very marrow is provided by the Christian faith and Christ is encountered at the summit. Bonaventure's argument for the paramount status of grace is pithy and neat. Happiness consists in the fruition of the highest good. As the highest good transcends the natural level in which man finds himself ensconced, it follows that happiness is impossible unless he is able to rise above himself. Man cannot accomplish this by himself and hence requires a superior force to elevate him. This superior force is grace which is given to those who request it humbly and devoutly.

Bonaventure refers to Denis as a "master of prayer" who prepares us *ad excessus mentales*[25] for mystical ecstasy; prayer itself is the "mother and ground" of *sursumactionis,* infused contemplation. The journey which takes man in the desired direction is comparable to the three days' journey into the wilderness of Exodus 3:18, and to a journey with three stages: afternoon, morning, and noonday. These three stages correspond to the threefold mode of existence found in things: in matter, in the human mind, and in the eternal art. Bonaventure embroiders the theme. The stages also correspond to the three "substances" in Christ and to the three aspects of the human soul.

The human soul has the following aspects: sensuality, turned to the exterior world; spirit, turned towards itself; and mind (*mens*), turned towards realities superior to itself.[26] These three aspects of the soul correspond to the threefold mode of existence found in things. The soul, then, with the help of Christ, will be able to rise up through these levels to their uncreated Source. But it must remain firm in its resolution to love God with its whole mind, heart, and soul, a disposition identified by Bonaventure with Christian wisdom, *sapientia christiana*.[27]

The three above mentioned levels are now doubled by Bonaventure as each of them can be considered either directly in itself or indirectly in relation to God. In this manner, he arrives at six stages which symbolize the number of days in which God created the world. Three crops up again in the three types of theology by which Christ taught "the science of truth": symbolical theology, theology proper, and mystical theology. The first, symbolical, deals with the correct use of sensible things; the second, theology proper, with intelligible entities; and the third, the mystical, elevates man to ecstasy, *supermentalis excessus*.[28] In order to engage in this enterprise it is necessary for man to exercise his natural powers, perfect them by means of prayer, through a holy life to receive justice, through meditation to arrive at "illuminating knowledge," and through contemplation to receive "perfecting wisdom." The journey of the mind to God is found encapsulated in this sentence.

Bonaventure advises the soul to pass from the sensible world to the Father after the manner of the Hebrews entering the promised land. With great care he enumerates the attributes of the physical world which reflect divine light. Like Augustine, Bonaventure points to the weight, number, and measure of things, their substance, power, and operations. From these "vestiges" the soul is able to elevate itself to the understanding of the power, wisdom, and goodness of the Creator.[29] Enthusiastically, he discovers the presence of God within creation by the manifestation of his attributes in the material order. That his intentions are more than speculative is evidenced by a rhetorical flourish at the ending of the first chapter of the *Itinerarium* which reflects an apologetical design. He takes to task those men who, after witnessing such a multiplicity of clues pointing to the divine presence, still fail to acknowledge it. They are no less than fools and are advised to make an effort to see what is truly present before the world itself rises up in anger against them.[30]

In the second chapter of the *Itinerarium,* Bonaventure launches into a rather tiresome epistemological discussion. He begins by distinguishing between the proper and common objects of sensation, in Aristotelian fashion, then moves to the discussion of the intelligences (angels) which rule the celestial spheres through the motion of bodies.[31] It is difficult if not impossible for modern man to put himself mentally in the place of Bonaventure vis-à-vis the understanding of the universe. He would have to disregard some of his most precious basic assumptions as well as enter into an alien world-image comprised of fixed stars, spheres, the *primum mobile,* and complicated structure of epicycles and eccentric cycles. It is advisable if not courageous to pass these speculations by except when they are essential to the understanding of the point at hand.

In any event, his remarks which are properly epistemological are clearer and more to the point. Bonaventure observes that sense-knowledge takes place through the medium of the *species* (likenesses) of things which generate pleasure in the knower, pleasure which is grounded on proportion and harmony. Beauty itself is harmonious symmetry.[32] Following sensation and the pleasure produced by it comes judgment which pronounces that the reason for the delectability of knowledge is *"proportio aequalitatis"*, a principle which transcends the physical order. Being immutable and spiritual, it belongs to another domain.[33] Here we find a faint echo of the Platonic Ideas in line with the discussion of equality in the *Phaedo*.

Although it may seem that Bonaventure has taken us on an epistemological fishing expedition, in reality he is making several important points. The very fact that all things have the power to generate *species* (likenesses), on being perceived, proclaims the eternal generation of the Word, as the very delight which the *species* produces in the knower is a faint reflection of its divine paradigm.[34] If this seems rather far-fetched it is probably because of our lack of familiarity with a symbolical vision of reality. If the peculiar temptation of medieval Aristotelianism was to radically demythologize the world and deprive it of its symbolical meaning, they initiated the trend of which we are the beneficiaries—that of medieval Augustinianism was to reduce the world to a filmy barrier between the human soul and God, notable mainly because of its nuisance value. Bonaventure moves in this latter direction, convinced as he was that ignorance of the symbolic meaning of things betrays ignorance concerning their natural properties.

God is the infallible standard of human judgment. These laws or standards are uncreated and pre-exist in the Eternal Art. It is understood that the Father creates through the Son (Word), who contains eternally the ideas of all things. It follows that things are signs, imperfect copies of a higher reality, which are provided by God to enable the human soul to rise from the sensible to the intelligible order, from the sign to the reality signified.[35] All things signify the invisible perfections of God as he is the origin, exemplar, and end of all creation. But all things do not signify God equally. Bonaventure accords a privileged status to those things which Scripture uses to symbolize spiritual realities, to act as theophanies, or as sacramental signs.[36] This section, which is basically a speculative commentary on

Romans 1:20, ends with the soul entering consciousness, "the mirror of the soul," where the Trinitarian image resides.

Possibly in the wake of Augustine's arguments in *De Civitate Dei* and elsewhere in which he discovers apodictic truth in the triadic form of existence, knowledge of existence, and love,[37] Bonaventure indicates that both knowledge and memory are grounded in self-love.[38] He refers to the triad of memory, understanding, and will, which, again following Augustine's lead, constitutes the soul as the image of God. He insists that the attentive consideration of these faculties will enable the soul to approach God, to "see" him in the manner described by St. Paul, *"per speculum in aenigmitate"* (1 Cor. 13:12). Not only is the Holy Trinity mirrored in the interworkings of memory, understanding, and will, but each individual faculty also mirrors the Trinity in its own way.

Memory, for example, retains past, present, and future through recollection, reception, and foresight. It also retains simple things such as the principles and axioms of the sciences (e.g., the whole is greater than any of its parts). Memory is then an image of eternity, the indivisible presence of which extends to all times. It contains *"invariabilium veritatum"*, immutable truths, and must therefore have present within itself an "unchangeable light" through which they are recalled. Through the consideration of memory, the human soul reveals itself as the image and likeness of God.[39]

More acute is the argument which Bonaventure applies to the understanding. He begins with the premise that the necessary precondition of knowledge is the comprehension of the meaning of the terms which are used in argument. This meaning is arrived at through definition. Now, the definition of a term is given by means of more universal terms, and these through even more universal terms, until the most universal terms are reached on which all the preceding are grounded. The most general of all terms is being-in-itself (*ens a se*). It follows that without knowledge of the most general term, being-in-itself, it is impossible to fully comprehend the definition of any particular thing.

Moreover, being-in-itself cannot be known without its properties being known: unity, truth, and goodness (*unum, verum, bonum*). The human mind cannot arrive at an exhaustive knowledge of created things without the knowledge of that simple Eternal Being in which the principles of all things are found *"in sua puritate."* Put another way: knowledge demands apodicticity. Neither the corporeal world nor the human mind can guarantee it. Immutable truth can be seen only in the true light which is the Word of God (Jn. 1:1-9).[40]

The will is exercised in deliberation, judgment, and desire. Deliberation inquires which is better, this or that, but the better cannot be known without possessing knowledge of the best. It follows that the notion of the Highest Good must be imprinted on the soul of whoever deliberates. Judgment requires an appeal to a standard or law by which it judges, a standard which transcends the human mind which appeals to it. As there is nothing superior to the human mind except its Creator, it follows that the will, when it appeals to a standard superior to itself, touches on the Divine Law.[41] Finally, desire moves by what it most loves and it most loves happiness. But happiness is not attained until the ultimate good is possessed. Hence, desire requires the Supreme Good without which nothing can be desired.

Collecting the strands of these arguments, Bonaventure indicates that memory leads to eternity, understanding to truth, and will to the Supreme Good.[42] He insists that the consideration of their origin, order and interrelatedness leads to the Trinity itself. Furthermore, even the sciences move in this direction. Philosophy is comprised of natural, rational, and moral disciplines. Natural philosophy investigates the cause of existence and leads to the power of the Father; rational philosophy deals with the basis of understanding and leads to the wisdom of the Son; and moral philosophy is concerned with the structure of life and leads to the goodness of the Holy Spirit.

The speculative atmosphere of these arguments is unabashedly Augustinian with strong Platonic resonances. The weakest parts resemble a running commentary on what was called the argument through degrees of perfection and reflected in Thomas Aquinas' *quarta via.* Bonaventure has the Eternal Law transmitting the certain and infallible rules of the sciences to the human mind through illumination. The presupposition which runs through these pages is that the human soul, if it has not lost its "sight" through sin, can be led to the contemplation of God through the consideration of itself.[43]

The preceding arguments take place mainly on a philosophical level. In contrast, the following stage of the journey is scripturally oriented and involves a further entry into oneself: a laborious task because of human weakness and the many temptations provided by the dispersion of the self in the world of things. Bonaventure's argument takes a theological direction: it would be impossible for man to elevate himself from the sensible world to co-intuition—a Bonaventurian term which signifies indirect knowledge—of Eternal Truth, if this Truth had not taken human form in Christ and constituted itself as intermediary.[44] God is attained only through Christ, not by means of natural reason no matter how excellent. The soul must be clothed with the theological virtues of faith, hope, and charity to be purified, illuminated, and perfected. In this manner the darkened image of God which is the human soul can be reconstituted and reformed in the likeness of the Heavenly Jerusalem.

Only in this way can the soul recover its "spiritual senses" and become, like the bride of the *Canticle,* properly disposed for ecstasy, *"disponitur anima ad mentales excessus."*[45] It becomes structured hierarchically in conformity with the exigencies of the Heavenly Jerusalem: purified, illuminated, and made perfect, disposed to those acts which correspond to the activities of the nine choirs of angels. The soul, by entering into itself, enters into the Heavenly Jerusalem and, in contemplating the angelic choirs, sees God indirectly.[46] We have been led from pondering on the natural operations of the human soul to the consideration of the divine perfections and from reflecting on the soul reformed by grace we have been elevated to God.

Two items will strike us as familiar. First the notion of hierarchy[47] which was encountered with almost perverse insistence in the *Corpus Areopagiticum.* Second, the triad of purification, illumination, and perfection, again roughly corresponding to the traditional division of the spiritual life. But there are marked differences between Bonaventure and Denis. The complex interrelationships in the Dionysian writings between the celestial and the ecclesiastical hierarchies is downplayed with Bonaventure focusing primarily on the relation between the celestial hierarchy and the individual soul. The first is viewed as possessing the model or paradigm which the individual soul is conscience-bound to reproduce. The *Itinerarium* contains an allusion to the blueprint of the Temple which God dictated to Moses in Exodus 26. Both Denis and Bonaventure seem to be following the scriptural tradition which views the unfolding of God's plan as the progressive dissemination on earth of the pattern of existence of the Heavenly Court. From the Christian viewpoint, the Incarnation marks the point at which the Wisdom by which God created the universe is made flesh and his Kingdom proclaimed.[48]

To repeat: the soul, aided by grace, is able to structure itself according to the specifications of the Heavenly Court and in this way become worthy to share in the divine life. In addition, the *Itinerarium* appears to subscribe to the view, common in the monastic circles of the early Middle Ages, which considered the *Parousia* not only as a communal event but one which takes place in the soul of the individual Christian. The third and fourth chapters of the *Itinerarium* suggest as much. The hierarchization of the soul is reflected in the natural order through illumination, viz., knowledge of those objective principles which ground both human thought and the physical world. The human mind is now able to "recollect" those eternal standards, "*regulae aeternae*," which are imprinted on it and proceed from the Eternal Art.

A small but troublesome point. Bonaventure has, thus far, referred to mystical experience only in a vague and general way. It seems that the *Itinerarium,* which Paul Vignaux called "the perfect union of scholasticism and mysticism,"[49] is singularly, suspiciously, devoid of mystical phenomena. This elicits further questions. Is the treatise fundamentally a theological or philosophical work? Is it an early attempt at a phenomenology of the spiritual life? Is the Franciscan inspiration one of content or merely one of style? After all, following Angel Clareno a case could be presented that it is simply an attempt to domesticate the original Franciscan spirit, which tended to the intense, enthusiastic, even wild. Or is it an example of genuine Franciscan piety interpreted by a methodical speculative mind of a very high order? Albeit at present rather precipitous, these questions should be kept in mind and deserve at very least a sincere effort at resolution.

The following two chapters, the fifth and sixth, are rather disappointing with mystical phenomena still on the horizon. In the Dionysian tradition, speculation seems to lead piety by the nose. Nevertheless, this segment contains a prolonged meditation, rationalistic though it be, on the names of God, with strong ties to the *Divine Names* and Anselm's *Proslogion.* The soul is now viewed allegorically as entering the Holy of Holies. The two cherubim of the Ark are interpreted as representing two different ways of contemplating the divine perfections which arise from the two "primary" names of God. The first, "He who is" originates in the Old Testament and proclaims the unity of the divine essence. The second, "the Good," originates in the New Testament and teaches the plurality of persons in the Godhead—the Trinity.[50] These names lead to a metaphysical excursus.

Being is apodictically certain. It is impossible to think that it does not exist. Pure Being can be understood only by negating non-being which, as it is itself a privation of being, can be thought only through the medium of being. This Pure Being which absolutely excludes non-being is Pure Act (*purus actus*) and is identified by Bonaventure with the Divine Being, God.[51] Nevertheless, he concedes that it is difficult to recognize this Divine Being even though it happens to be that without which absolutely nothing can be known. He likens the predicament to the eye which is so attentive to differences in color that it fails to see the light by which it sees all other things. Accustomed as the human mind is to the shadows of the material world, when it catches sight of the dazzling light of the Supreme Being it seems to see nothing. It is blinded by the excess of light, and fails to realize that this darkness is the supreme illumination of the human mind.[52]

At this point, Bonaventure seems to be balanced between Denis and Aristotle. He cites approvingly the II *Metaph.*, "eye of the bat" analogy but his argument evokes Parmenides rather than Denis or Aristotle, in its "unpacking" of the implications contained in Pure Being. It is primary, eternal, simple, in act, perfect, and one. These attributes are of such certainty that whoever understands being-in-itself (*ipsum esse*) cannot even think their opposite as each entails the other.[53] These attributes are contrasted, compared, juggled, and their interrelationships and permutations used to draw out additional perfections. After this somewhat convoluted and laborious interlude, Bonaventure concludes that Pure Being (*esse*) is the alpha and omega, origin and end, that it is eternal and omnipresent, containing and penetrating all durations. It is, in a phrase taken from Alan of Lille, "an intelligible sphere whose center is everywhere and circumference nowhere."[54]

In a daring extension of Anselm's *Proslogion* method, Bonaventure describes God as a good greater than which cannot be thought. He then takes a surprising leap, concluding from this description that God must be thought of as Trinity. The justification comes from the Dionysian principle "the good is diffusive of itself"[55] which he unpacks, perhaps somewhat arbitrarily, to conclude with a Lover, a Co-Lover, and a process of "spiration." To deny this conclusion would, in his opinion, entail a contradiction: the Highest Good would not be the Highest Good as it would not be diffusive to the highest degree. Furthermore, the diffusion of good in creation is a "mere point" compared to the immensity of Eternal Goodness. But even a greater degree of diffusion occurs when the one diffusing communicates to the other His very substance and nature.[56] Again, he arrives at the Trinity.

At this rarified height of speculation, Bonaventure, perhaps wary of intellectual vertigo, admonishes the reader against the danger of presumption: "do not believe that you can comprehend the incomprehensible." At the same time he urges him to greater devotion. Who, he asks, is not stirred to wonder by the sight of these marvels? Simply by lifting our eyes to the Highest Good it is possible to understand with certitude that all of them are comprised in the Holy Trinity. Through the meditation on the properties of the Trinity the soul is enabled to rise to contemplation.[57] Extending this meditation to include the union of God and man in the unique person of Christ will increase wonder/admiration to an even higher degree as will also meditation on the "inner life" of the persons of the Trinity.[58]

Bonaventure indicates that at this point the soul enjoys *perfect illumination* of the mind, (*perfectio illuminationis mentis*), as it contemplates in Christ the reduction of alpha and omega, circumference and center, Creator and creature, the book written within and the book written without. Although referring to Rev. 5:1 and Ezek. 2:9 what he has in mind is the speculative distinction between the divine ideas on the one hand and the physical world on the other. The soul reaches this level on the sixth stage of the journey. Only the seventh day remains.

The seventh day is the day of rest, the Eternal Sabbath, in which the human soul rests from all work and finally arrives at mystical ecstasy. The six previous stages are compared by Bonaventure to the six steps of Solomon's throne. Only one thing is lacking and the soul presses on to a further elevation in which Jesus Christ is seen to be the "way" and the "door," a mystery hidden in God from eternity.[59] Whoever concentrates the totality of his attention and affects on Christ crucified passes over the Red Sea from Egypt to the desert. There he shall taste the "hidden manna" and find rest with Christ, experiencing, as far as is possible in this life, the words of the Savior to the good thief, "Today you shall be with me in paradise" (Lk. 23:43).[60]

Spiritual perfection is linked to the Franciscan tradition. St. Francis is the model of perfect contemplation because of the sublime nature of his experience on Mount Alverna. But he is also—the disciple Bonaventure insists—the model of the active life as well. In the most specifically mystical passage yet, he insists that if the transition from the material world to God is to be perfect, all intellectual operations must be transcended and the apex of the affects (*apex affectus*) displaced and transformed into God: "*Hoc autem est mysticum et secretissimum.*"[61] At this point human industry ceases. Speculation ends while unction abounds, language ceases and inner joy overflows.

At the very threshold of infused contemplation, Bonaventure cites two passages from the *Mystical Theology*.[62] The first is the hieratic introductory prayer to the Trinity, the second the admonition to Timothy which, in effect, charts the path to the superessential Ray of Darkness. Unlike Denis, Bonaventure stresses the affective and supernatural character of the experience. Whoever is tempted to press speculation further is advised to "question" desire not understanding, grace not doctrine, prayer not study. The world of intellectual speculation has been left behind. It is Christ who kindles the fire that inflames man and carries him to God, a God who is not light but fire. Whoever reaches these heights lives a sort of death, a death by which he enters darkness, and passes with Christ crucified out of this world to the

Father. The *Itinerarium* ends with a scriptural hymn:

> My flesh and my heart have grown faint
>   You are the God of my heart
> and the God who is my portion forever
>   Blessed be the Lord forever
> and all the people will say:
>   Let it be: let it be
>   Amen.

Many questions arise. Does Bonaventure's mystic quest end at the point in which the method of detachment found in the *Mystical Theology* begins? The *Itinerarium* is certainly less intellectualistic than the *Mystical Theology* and greater emphasis is put on the affective aspect of mystical experience. Bonaventure uses detachment principally as an index to God's incomprehensibility. Moreover, although the ascent of the soul by several stages is hierarchical, it is scarcely an ascent through negations. Again, the domains of grace and nature are clearly, though perhaps not precisely, distinguished. A variety of impressive philosophical and theological moves are directed precisely at eliciting affective reactions.

But there certainly is a Neoplatonic aspect to the *Itinerarium*. The ascent is based on the proposition that thought about the highest things purifies the soul, transforms it, and gives it "spiritual wings" to ascend higher. Nevertheless, only the seventh chapter is properly mystical, although the sixth may well constitute a halfway house between the natural and supernatural after the manner of Teresa's fourth mansion. The elevation of the soul through admiration/ wonder is hardly mystical contemplation. It is more in line with speculative contemplation derived from classic *theoria*. Before the seventh chapter Bonaventure refers to grace without mentioning any possible experience.[63] In spite of this, the "higher contemplation" of the last chapter is clearly not generated by intellectual speculation but is given by God. Only the status of the sixth stage is in doubt. Although it is not mystical contemplation Bonaventure has words of praise for this "illumination." Why?

Oratio igitur est mater et origo sursumactionis.[64] Although he does not in fact make a clear distinction between nature and grace, rational speculation and prayer, argument and spiritual purification in the practical order, prayer is the point of departure and the very ground of this spiritual journey. He does clearly distinguish between ordinary and extraordinary, the spiritual and the properly mystical. Perhaps the *Itinerarium*, following Anselm's *Proslogion* (some might add Clement of Alexandria), is a praying in thought, at least until thought is transcended. The Bonaventurian conception of *sursumactio* suggests that grace is at work from the very beginning of the enterprise with the goal in view being to attain the perfect observance of the law and Christian wisdom which is reflected in the injunction found in Mk. 12:30, repeating Deuteronomy, to love God with our whole mind, heart, and soul.[65]

It is imperative that the rectitude of the soul which had been lost through original sin be recovered. This can be done only through Jesus Christ by means of the three "theologies": symbolical, dealing with material things; theology proper, dealing with intelligible things; and mystical, by means of which the human soul is lifted up to ecstasy.[66] Because of the paramount importance of prayer and the elevating function of the three "theologies" it would seem to follow that even though the seventh stage alone may be considered properly mystical, all the preceding stages, not only the sixth, must possess the ferment of supernatural life, the cause of the soul's elevation to ecstasy.

The difficulties presented by the *Itinerarium* are compounded by the notable absence of mystical phenomena. The phenomena cataloged by Father Marechal[67] some years ago are conspicuous by their absence. Details of the spiritual life are also absent, as are accounts of ascetical practices, devotional methods, types of prayer, and so on. The personal intensity of the *Confessions,* the Gothic exoticism of a Meister Eckhart, the psychological finesse of a John of the Cross are all foreign to Bonaventure. Even his genuine and moving Franciscan spirituality is circumscribed within the limits of theological prudence. As indicated previously, the peculiar dangers of the milieu would incline him against both over-enthusiastic spirituality and desiccated rationality. Bonaventure's thought may well be a domestication but hardly a perversion of the original Franciscan spirit.

Was he a mystic or merely a mystical writer? The question is simplistic and impossible to answer. Although many of his works are pious to the extent of being maudlin—at least by contemporary standards—a work of the caliber of the *Incendium Amoris* merits comparison with the commentaries of John of the Cross. Bonaventure was a pious Christian and a medieval one at that. He was not a "pilgrim of the Absolute," philosophical or otherwise in the manner of Plotinus, Proclus, and possibly Denis the Areopagite. He was ensconced within a Christian tradition which was passing through some decidedly hard times. The method adopted in the *Itinerarium* of interrogating the physical world and man through the dual prisms of nature and grace is ingenious but not original. The journey of the soul described through a tapestry of speculations which gain in depth and richness is impressive. His final appeal to the *Mystical Theology* is a tribute to the authority of Denis. Though it could be interpreted as a mere disclaimer of personal responsibility it is perhaps his way of giving notice that the limits of the thinkable have been passed.

The *Itinerarium* is exceptional in most categories, as a spiritual, theological, and philosophical work. It is not phenomenology of the spiritual life as it dispenses with the particulars of worship and the religious life which would be of prime importance to a study of this type. But it can be said to adumbrate the Husserlian epochē, a fact which has not escaped the notice of contemporary phenomenologists. An early commentator was probably on the right track when he entitled the work *Liber de investigatione Creatoris per creaturas* as it is, in effect, a study or investigation of the Creator through the medium of creatures. It is a sustained and disciplined attempt to manifest the reality of things—things as they are vis-à-vis God—an effort to unveil the theophanic presence in the world. In the *Itinerarium*, Bonaventure stands at the threshold between the intellectualism of Denis and the devotional, practical mysticism of Teresa of Avila.

Epilogue

The influence of Bonaventure's thought on the later Middle Ages was substantial especially within the confines of the Franciscan Order.

Matthew of Aquasparta, John Peckham of the Oxford condemnations of 1277, William de la Mare, Roger Marston, and Peter John Olivi were all inspired to some degree by his works; Ramón Lull also, insomuch as anyone could influence this eccentric wanderer. After the fourteenth century his influence lapses although he continued to have distinguished admirers if not adepts. Spirituality owes him a considerable debt. Even Savonarola was impressed and wrote a laudatory commentary of the *Incendium Amoris*.[68] When Pope Leo XIII inaugurated the resuscitation of Catholic philosophy about a century ago, Bonaventure was placed after Thomas Aquinas. Even a tenuous line of affiliation to modernity has been well represented. Rosmini, Gatry, and Blondel recognized his presence in their works. It seems that whenever an appeal is made in the direction of Augustine, Bonaventure is also addressed.

Affective spirituality in particular owes much to him. One of his works was at one time ascribed to the English mystic, Richard Rolle, and the Counter-Reformation writer on spirituality, Dom Augustine Baker, thought highly of his spiritual works.[69] He has been considered the principal link between the monastic spirituality of St. Bernard and that of the *Imitation of Christ*.[70] When meditation on the humanity of Christ is given a prominent status his influence is often present. Bonaventure reached Spain through the Abbot of Montserrat, Dom Garcia Jimenez de Cisneros, who had eight hundred copies of the *Incendium Amoris* printed under the name of *Parvum Bonum*.[71] It is possible that through this work, as well as other sources, the Bonaventurian influence might have touched Ignatius of Loyola and Teresa of Avila. It is entirely in character that Dante has Bonaventure—*l'amor che me fa bella*—delivering a eulogy of St. Dominic.[72]

But in retrospect, his enemies seem to have won the day. The Latin Averroists were merely a beachhead of a wider movement towards secularization. The enclave of theology-free rationality was able to extend itself until the sixteenth century mathematization of nature severed human culture from its roots in religious faith. The religious domain, cut off from the great human enterprises, was left to drift in the ether of emotionalism and private interpretation. The Book of Nature was severed from the Book of Scripture. Although the Franciscan *Zelanti* were put to flight and ultimately rooted out, the struggle left permanent scars.

They were able to displace their intense enthusiasm and fervid imagination on to the secular field. If they could not transform the world by means of the spirit, they would do so through material means: science, exploration, revolution. The Eternal Gospel suffered a radical sea-change. Catharism also disappeared, at least as a mass movement, but has remained a temptation to a humanity yet to recover title to the earthly paradise. It has surfaced in sporadic bursts since the Middle Ages and with exceptional individuals such as William Blake. Perhaps most important, it is a subliminal malaise which has found far-reaching expression in the politics of modernity.

Bonaventure attempted to preserve Christian teachings from those who would discard them for the dictates of Aristotelian physics or the call of an alien God. He fought against those in his own Order who would exchange traditional Christianity for a messianic counterpart of wondrous promise but suspect origin. In these endeavors he was supported by an intellectual ground derived principally from Augustine. Bonaventure was able—no small task—to buttress a foundation become shaky while contributing to the permanent things. He was at times overzealous, even harsh.[73] The tradition which has Bonaventure and Thomas Aquinas fast friends at Paris might have been meant to palliate their fundamental disagreements.[74] His aversions were instinctual and profound, his attitude to Aristotle a case in point.

Like the miraculous larks in his *Legenda maior* who, in spite of their love of light and hatred of twilight, come at twilight to give glory to the deceased St. Francis,[75] Bonaventure praised God through his works in spite of the difficulties he encountered. In this way he was able to rise above historical circumstance, the clamor of debate, and the deadening gravity of public opinion. One of the many medieval theologians who attempted to fuse the rationalistic spirituality of Denis with the affective stance of the day, he succeeded better than most. By holding Franciscan piety within the bounds of theological reason, he was able to neutralize its anarchic tendencies and in so doing constitute a vigorous tradition in the history of spirituality.

NOTES

[1]Refer to L. Bouyer, J. Leclercq, F. Vandenbroucke, *The Spirituality of the Middle Ages,* trans. by the Benedictines of Holme Eden Abbey, (London: Burns & Oates, 1968), pp. 243-261. Friedrich Heer, *The Medieval World,* trans. by J. Sondheimer, (New York: Mentor, 1962), esp. pp. 157-234.

[2]Edgar de Bruyne, *Estudios de Estética Medieval,* trans. by A. Suarez, (Madrid: Editorial Gredos, 1958), vol. III, pp. 214-265.

[3]Heer, *op. cit.,* p. 209. Refer also to Steven Runciman, *The Medieval Manichee,* (Cambridge: Cambridge Univ. Press, 1960), esp. pp. 116-170.

[4]Refer to Heer, *op. cit.,* pp. 157-196.

[5]See Majorie Reeves, *Joachim of Fiore and the Prophetic Future,* (New York: Harper & Row, 1977). For additional material refer to *Joachim of Fiore in Christian Thought: Essays on the Influence of the Calabrian Prophet,* ed. by D. West, (Philadelphia: Ben Franklin Press, 1976).

[6]*Concordia,* V8. 112. Cited by G. Fraile, *Historia de la filosofia,* (Madrid: BAC 1960), vol. II, pp. 541-542.

[7]These principal works of Joachim are: *Concordia Veteris et Novi Testamenti, Expositio in Apocalypsim,* and the *Psalterium decem chordarum.*

[8]A fairly good sketch of Bonaventure's life and work is given by Ephrem Longpré, "Bonaventure, St." *Dictionnaire d'histoire et geographie ecclesiastiques,* (Paris, 1937), vol. IX, cols. 741-788. A brief study of his philosophical thought is provided by Armand Maurer, *Medieval Philosophy,* (New York: Random House, 1962), pp. 137-152. For a closer look, Etienne Gilson, *The Philosophy of St. Bonaventure,* trans. by I. Trethowan & F. J. Sheed, (London: Sheed & Ward, 1938), and Efrem Bettoni, *St. Bonaventure,* trans. by A. Gambatese, (Notre Dame: Univ. of Notre Dame Press, 1964). His works are given in the *Opera Omnia,* 10 vols., Quaracchi, 1882-1902. The present study relies on the bilingual (Latin/Spanish) edition of his principal works, *Obras de San Buenaventura,* directed and introduced by L. Amoros, B. Aperribay, and M. Oromi, 5 vols., (Madrid: BAC, 1948). The English translation of the *Itinerarium* is provided by Ewart Cousins in *Bonaventure,* (New York: Paulist Press, 1978).

[9]Refer to Longpré, *op. cit.,* col. 761ff.

[10]*Cronica,* I, pp. 294, 301-302.

[11]*Historia,* I, p. 277.

[12]*Ibid.,* I, p. 285.

[13]Heer, *op. cit.,* p. 149.

[14]*De reductione art.,* no. 26.

[15]*Christus, Unum Omnium . . .*, 2, 6, 11.

[16]A. Maurer, *op. cit.*, p. 140.

[17]*Itinerarium*, IV, 2, (Eng. trans. p. 88).

[18]*Christus, Unum Omnium*, 15.

[19]*Itinerarium*, I, 6, (p. 62).

[20]*Ibid.*, Prol. 2, (p. 54).

[21]*Ibid.*, Prol. 3, (p. 54).

[22]*Christus, Unum Omnium*, 16-17.

[23]*De scientia Christi*, 4.

[24]*Itinerarium*, Prol. 3, (p. 55).

[25]*Ibid.*, I, 1, (p. 60).

[26]*Ibid.*, I, 3-4, (p. 61).

[27]*Ibid.*, I, 4, (p. 61).

[28]*Ibid.*, I, 7, (pp. 62-63).

[29]*Ibid.*, I, 11, (p. 64).

[30]*Ibid.*, I, 15, (p. 68).

[31]*Ibid.*, II, 3, (pp. 70-71).

[32]*Ibid.*, II, 5, (pp. 71-72).

[33]*Ibid.*, II, 6, (p. 72).

[34]*Ibid.*, II, 7-8, (pp. 72-73).

[35]*Ibid.*, II, 11, (p. 76).

[36]*Ibid.*, II, 12, (p. 77).

[37]*De Civitate Dei*, XI, 26.

[38]*Itinerarium*, III, 1, (pp. 79-80).

[39]*Ibid.*, II, 2, (pp. 80-81).

[40]*Ibid.*, III, 3, (p. 82).

[41]*Ibid.*, III, 4, (p. 83).

[42]*Ibid.*, III, 4, (p. 84).

[43]*Ibid.*, III, 6-7, (pp. 84-86).

[44]*Ibid.*, IV, 2, (pp. 87-88).

[45]*Ibid.*, IV, 3, (p. 89).

[46]*Ibid.*, IV, 4, (p. 90).

[47]*Ibid.*, IV, 7, (pp. 92-93).

[48]A random sampling would include Rom. 8:1-39, Col. 3:1-4, and Rev. 21. For precedents see Ezek. 1-3; 10-11 and Ex. 25:40.

[49]Paul Vignaux, *Philosophy in the Middle Ages*, trans. by E. C. Hall, (Cleveland: The World Publishing Co., 1962), p. 112.

[50]*Itinerarium*, V, 2, (p. 95).

[51]*Ibid.*, V, 2, (p. 96).

[52]*Ibid.,* V, 4, (pp. 96-97).

[53]*Ibid.,* V, 5-6, (pp. 97-98).

[54]*Ibid.,* V, 7, (pp. 99-101).

[55]*De cael. hier.,* IV, 1; *De div. nom.,* IV, 1, 20.

[56]*Itinerarium,*VI, 2, (p. 103).

[57]*Ibid.,* VI, 3, (pp. 105-106).

[58]*Ibid.,* VI, 6, (pp. 107-108).

[59]*Ibid.,* VII, 1, (pp. 110-111).

[60]*Ibid.,* VII, 2, (pp. 111-112).

[61]*Ibid.,* VII, 4, (p. 113).

[62]*Ibid.,* VII, 5, (pp. 114-115).

[63]*Ibid.,* VI, 6, (pp. 102-103).

[64]*Ibid.,* I, 1, (p. 60).

[65]Refer to Mk. 12:30; Matt. 22:37; Lk. 10:37.

[66]*Itinerarium* I, 7, (pp. 62-63).

[67]Joseph Maréchal, *Studies in the Psychology of the Mystics,* trans. by A. Thorold, (Albany: Magi Books, 1964), pp. 147-216.

[68]*Obras de San Buenaventura,* vol. 4, p. 89.

[69]See David Knowles, *The English Mystical Tradition,* (New York: Harper & Row, 1961), pp. 48, 175.

[70]Refer to Dom Francis Vanderbroucke, "The Franciscan Spring" in *Spirituality,* p. 310.

[71]*Obras de San Buenaventura,* vol. IV, p. 91, note 4.

[72]*Divina Commedia,* Canto 12, 31ff.

[73]A good example is *In Haexaem.,* II, 7; V, 21; XIX, 12, *et al.*

[74]Refer to my "An Episode in Medieval Aristotelianism: Maimonides and St. Thomas on the Active Intellect," *The Thomist,* Vol. 47, No. 3, pp. 317-338, esp. 331-335.

[75]*Legenda maior,* 14, 6, (Eng. trans. p. 320).

III
Ramón Lull

In 1239 Pope Gregory IX issued a condemnation of the Talmud on the grounds that it deviated from the biblical heritage of the Old Testament. On June 20 of the following year he instructed the Bishop of Paris—the theologian William of Auvergne—and the superiors of the Mendicant Orders to burn any of the books found to contain doctrinal error. After several proceedings twenty or so wagonloads of manuscripts were burned at the Place de la Grève. A few years later, in 1244, Pope Innocent IV asked King Louis IX to burn those copies of the Talmud which had survived. The Jews appealed to Rome, a Legatine Tribunal was established, the evidence was reviewed, and the guilty verdict upheld.[1] In these proceedings Talmudic Judaism was opposed to biblical Judaism and the Talmud viewed as the principal cause of the Jewish rejection of Christianity. Allegiance to the Talmud was interpreted as precluding obedience to the Torah. Furthermore, as the Legatine Tribunal stated, the Jews presented an alien presence in Christian society and a clear threat to the faith which should be addressed.[2]

This condemnation reflected a novel conception of the place of the Jews in Christendom, one at odds with Augustine's view, by this time traditional, that Jews were entitled to a definite albeit circumscribed place in society. Their staunch adherence to the Old Testament was viewed as a witness to the truth and historicity of Christ. Moreover, the conversion of the Jews was foretold by St. Paul. In spite of the severity of his usual charges against the Jews—blindness, hardness of heart, pride, and infidelity—Augustine considered them to be a "figure" of the Christian people, depositaries and custodians of Scripture for the benefit of the Gentiles, and witnesses, no matter if reluctant, to the truth of the Christian faith.[3] He insisted that the books of the Jews "our enemies" contained the truths of Christ and the Church. They were dispersed and not exterminated so that they could disseminate the "prophecies of grace" throughout the world and in this way help to convert the infidel. If the Jews had in fact rejected Holy Scripture, they would have perished along with the rites of the Temple.[4]

Augustine's views provided an opening which later Christian apologists would use to advantage in making their attack on the oppressed people. The Jews, they stated, had distanced themselves from Scripture and therefore had lost their place in Christian society. Having lost their rights due to the seduction of the Talmud the Jews became, as it were, fair game. This conception nurtured the worst anti-Jewish polemic which was reflected in the outbreak of violence from the thirteenth century on.[5] Needless to say, a Hitlerian "final solution" was not contemplated but rather conversion, hopefully *en masse*, a pious hope which inspired some of the less benign chapters of medieval history. Although the full responsibility for the persecutions can be assigned only to the unfortunate convergence of a multiplicity of factors, there is no doubt that the religious and intellectual leadership was provided, in the main, by the Mendicant Orders, at least by those Dominicans and Franciscans who subscribed to the new interpretation of Jewish status.

A growing awareness of the potential danger of Judaism as a proselytizing force, whether based on reality or folklore, helped to fuel this unfortunate state of affairs. The Papal pronouncements against Christian converts to Judaism began with Pope Clement IV's *In turbato corde* of 1267 which was followed by admonitions by Gregory X, Nicholas III, Nicholas IV, and others. The hatred generated by the polemic in the Jewish community is evidenced by an early circular letter (1232-33) addressed to the Jewish communities in Spain which refers in unflattering terms to "the deceived and deceiving Minorites ...(and)...the squeaking and gibbering Preachers."[6]

But evangelization proceeded apace with the new conception of Jewish presence and became the task entrusted to the Mendicant Orders. Some of the leaders were converted Jews, with the effort probably reaching its apogee in the treatises of Nicholas of Lyra and in the *Pugio fidei* of Ramon Martí, a former disciple of Albertus Magnus and fellow student of Thomas Aquinas. The "grey eminence" of this aggressive missionary enterprise was Ramon de Penyafort, a Dominican, sometime confessor to Pope Gregory IX and Master General of the Order. A careful scholar, Penyafort was responsible for editing a collection of *Decretales* promulgated by that Pope, and for instituting a revision of the Dominican constitutions. More to the point perhaps, he was instrumental in establishing the Inquisition in the kingdom of Aragon and encouraged Thomas Aquinas to compose his *Summa Contra Gentiles* as an intellectual aid in the conversion of the non-Christian world. He also founded Dominican houses of study at Tunis, Murcia, Jativa, Valencia, and Barcelona to teach Hebrew and Arabic. Tradition has him cooperating with Alfonso X of Castile in the composition of the *Partidas*. The strands of both medieval greatness and prejudice come together in his person. He would communicate his vision to a fellow Catalan, Ramón Lull, and be instrumental in shaping his rather wild and eccentric talents.

Lull has been accused of attempting to bring the anti-Jewish ideology of the Friars to its ultimate conclusion.[7] This accusation, it must be admitted, has some foundation in fact. Lull's feverish imagination enthusiastically framed enterprises to hasten the advent of a universal Christian *respublica* through the conversion of the "infidel." He was close to the Dominicans, then closer still to the Franciscans. In this he reminds us of another turbulent visionary of an earlier era, Roger Bacon. It should be expected that his apostolic zeal, whatever may be said of his order of priorities, would be reflected in his spirituality. The vicissitudes of his peripatetic existence were etched on the deeper regions of his soul.

Background

Although the problem of the identity of Pseudo-Denis is intellectually stimulating, the *Corpus Areopagiticum* belongs to a rarefied domain in which individuality is somehow crass. The work of Ramón Lull cannot be comprehended apart from his life. The tortuous permutations of his Art—a sort of medieval computing machine—the richness of his allegory, and the naivete of his speculations must be viewed with his life as backdrop. More than Denis, Bonaventure, and even more than Teresa of Avila, Lull is a reflection of his age. Its virtues, vices, and values are found in him magnified and somewhat distorted.

His life spanned the thirteenth and the first years of the fourteenth centuries (1232-1316). He deserved the epithet which he used as the title of a late work, the *Phantasticus*. He viewed himself as "the most fantastic of the fantastic" and was not far from the truth. The epithet certainly reflected contemporary opinion. The testimony of his age bequeathed to posterity a fabulous picture of Lull as the author of well over a thousand works—he wrote from 150-200—together with a lovely, truly poignant death scene which unfortunately is probably apocryphal. The mortally injured Ramón expires in a small fishing boat after finally catching a last glimpse of his exquisite Majorca. The age also left a heritage of controversy. The Inquisitor, Nicholas Eymeric, pursued his memory with rarely equalled persistence and venom.

Ramón Lull[8] was the child of the superficial and sensual culture of his native Majorca which inherited, at least to some degree, the carnal mystique of the Provencal "courts of love" and the self-righteous puritanism of the Cathars. Catalonia and Majorca had become the refuge of Franciscan Spirituals and Joachimites of all stripes. Voluptuousness of color and form found an uncomfortable neighbor in the fanaticism of the Pure, while an aristocratic notion of status struggled with the harsh, leveling asceticism of the Perfect. These trends found their reflection in Lull. If a fairly safe generalization is allowable, it is even today reflected to some extent in the people of Catalonia in their unusual synthesis of practical expertise and high romanticism.

As many of the saints found in medieval hagiography, Ramón Lull was converted through a vision—actually a series of visions—from a profligate life to one of sanctity. He was married at the time, although he was still in search of romantic adventures at Majorca and Montpellier. He would later go into detail regarding his infatuation with women. One day he was writing lyrics to a melody addressed to his latest *amour* when he looked up and saw the figure of the crucified Christ on his right side, *veé nostre senyor Déu Jesucrist penjant en creu*.[9] He buckled and left the room precipitously. A week later, again writing a poem, he again became aware of this unsettling presence. Alarmed, he buried his head in his bedclothes.[10] The vision continued to pursue him and the reluctant courtier's conversion is dated from the fifth and last such vision. Some years later, during one of those emotional nadirs which plagued him throughout his life, Lull, in his *Desconhort*, recalls in verse how Jesus had rescued him from his sensuality (*carnalitat*) by means of five visions, adding that the purpose of these visions was to remind him of God so that he would love him and endeavor to make him known throughout the world.[11] This he indeed attempted to do with singular zeal throughout his legendary life.

But the fantastic and illusory in Lull goes hand in hand with the practical and farsighted. His luxuriant fantasy coalesces rather haphazardly with a logic unmerciful in its rigor. After a preparation of several years spent mainly in the study of Arabic, Lull began to debate on home ground with the Jews and Moslems of Palma and wrote his first book, the *Llibre de Contemplació* (Book of Contemplation), in Arabic. He was forty years old at the time. Lull had wished to attend the University of Paris but was dissuaded from his purpose by Ramon de Penyafort.

In the *Llibre de Contemplació* he is already preoccupied with the conversion of Arabs and Jews and lists the major stumbling blocks which they find to conversion: the doctrines of the Trinity, Incarnation, Christ's divinity, and the Virgin birth head the account. More important, no less than forty-six chapters are dedicated to love and the important terms *amic* (Lover) and *amat* (Beloved). This was followed by the *Llibre del Gentil e los Tres Savis* (Book of the Gentile and the Three Wise Men) in which the Gentile, a heathen philosopher facing death, sets out on a journey in which he meets three sages, a Jew, a Christian, and a Moslem, each of which present their case to him. Unlike Judah Halevi's *Kuzari*, which may well have influenced Lull, it is not stated which of the three faiths the protagonist finally embraces although, predictably, the Christian argument is the strongest.

In this work we find the first example of Lull's unique style. He places the arguments of the three wise men within an objective framework taking the exotic form of five trees with a combined total of 179 flowers, an allegory which represents the divine attributes and their possible combinations with both "created virtues" and the seven deadly sins.[12] The sages take their lead from this scheme and frame their arguments accordingly. Although it has the negligible charm of a Rubic's cube it provides a framework for the argument, a common ground in rational discourse which must be adhered to by the three participants.

This tendency to search for a common ground in natural reason, to delight in complex permutations and combinations, was confirmed in a decisive experience which Lull believed was a divine illumination. It provided him with the order and form to compose books against the errors of the "infidel."[13] This took place on the eighth day of a retreat on Mount Randa near Palma. Ramón—one can only with great difficulty imagine his euphoria—went down to the Cistercian monastery of La Real and there composed his *Ars Magna*, or Great Art, which was to provide him with the method of most of his early works, one to which he came to attribute nearly miraculous powers. To the end of his days Lull believed in its universal efficacy and never really came to terms with its rejection by the intellectual community.

The *Art* is difficult to comprehend and as a result is impossible to duplicate successfully. Beginning with the supreme categories of thought, the fundamental concepts, he attempts to arrive at truth by means of the combination of concepts which progressively become more complex. In other words, Lull is attempting to deduce the laws applicable to contingent being from the *dignitatis divinae*, the divine attributes. Moving from the very first principles to those which serve to define the different sciences, his *combinatoria* issues into a system of concepts which is intended to possess both logical and metaphysical relevance. Perhaps in this way adumbrating Leibniz, truth is identified with whatever assures the maximum of harmony between the Creator and his creation. This Art is expressed through geometric figures which form concentric circles that represent God, at the center, the divine attributes, humanity, and the world. The possible combinations are indicated on tables symbolized by letters of the alphabet, out of which Lull composed a sort of algebraic logic.

This Art is supposed to provide the answer to any and all problems. Lull sincerely believed that it was a God-given grace destined to promote the glory of God by means of the conversion of the "infidel." To an unmathematical mind, one devoid of the pathos of numbers who feels no emotional links to the Pythagoreans, the Art is no more than an ingenious but unbearably ponderous game of concepts, numbers, and letters of dubious applicability. It has been called a cybernetic machine, a computing engine, a thinking machine, mental alchemy, and more. Its very possibility rests on Lull's ingenuous belief that all things have an exact transcription in language and that a rigorous method which is able to determine the combinations of concepts, will also determine the combinations of things. With his usual enthusiastic optimism concerning the Art, he assigned six months of study for its proper comprehension. Still, he must have had second thoughts as sometime after he wrote *The Art of Finding Truth* and still later composed an *Application of the "Art General"* and a resumé of the method called the *Ars Brevis*, all of which attempt to simplify the original formulation.

A glimpse into the presuppositions of the Art is given by a work with the unpromising name of the *Book of the Order of Chivalry*. Lull indicates that each state of life—"calling," "office"—has an appropriate meaning which entails specific duties. The office of clerk, knight, priest, and so on, are given in a hierarchical order which would have delighted the author of the *Corpus Areopagiticum*. Each task has its place in the edifice. But the men and women who fail to live up to the Creator's original intent in establishing these classes—and this seems to be the majority—pervert the meaning of the office which they hold. To live according to the exigencies expressed within the concept of each office becomes a project of wholesale reform which also leads to the rediscovery of the true meaning of each office. It demands a molding of each person's life within the exigencies specified by the concept which expresses each office, as the concept articulates its objective structure. This is to say, the concept demands existential fulfillment in the life of the person involved.

As Lull believes that language adequately expresses things, it follows that any gap between the two—between the concept and the thing it expresses—must indicate both a logical and a moral flaw. This may well explain the consistent and somewhat heavy-handed use of allegory. In his view the metaphor expresses the concept in a plastic manner and is therefore an extension of the thing which it describes.

In this manner the apparent lacuna between allegory and logical demonstration, emotion, and dialectic, may be bridged. No matter how extravagant the image or outlandish the narrative—many taken from Arabic sources—they move in accordance with the harmony within, the logic which undergirds it. The very exuberance of the images is in this way grounded on the precision of the system. Small wonder that Leibniz had kind words for Lull and considered him the discoverer of the *ars combinatoria*. Today, we can consider him as the distant precursor of the computer.

The illumination of Mount Randa set Ramón Lull off on a public life which was to span over forty years and take him beyond the limits of the world known to Europeans of his day. He was the first European to describe the Sudan, Abyssinia, Turkey, and Georgia and his apocryphal travels were even more extensive. Fueling his urgency was his fervent desire to reduce all the languages of the world to one common language and through this reduction to convert the "infidel" and bring about the desired unity of mankind. He aspired to a universal Catholic Christianity. His travels, enterprises, wild schemes, and wilder fantasies, were all directed to this end. Ramón, in his pathetic *Desconhort*, laments that the Art is rejected, very few understand or esteem it, in a world which is out of kilter, *lo món no és en bo estat*.[14] But he believes that the world can be put in order, through the common ground of natural reason, by means of the Art. Here, Lull can reasonably be considered to anticipate those secular schemes for the rehabilitation of reason which will proliferate in the seventeenth century and find their highest expression in Descartes' *Regulae* and Spinoza's *De Enmendatione Intellectus*.

Lull's tragedy is that even his most practical and best formulated plans went awry. Even his prestige as one-time courtier and friend of kings waned with time. His pet project, the missionary college at Miramar for the study of Arabic established by James II, was mysteriously abandoned some fifteen years after its foundation. His many visits to Rome, where, as is to be expected, he was lavish and insistent with advice, proved to be futile. His missionary interventions in Africa have a chiaroscuro character and, as far as can be ascertained, were not very successful. His bouts with depression—the melancholy of the ancients—and his ruminations concerning sin and sensuality, ring true though somewhat morbid according to contemporary taste. The account of his choice of habit—it was Franciscan—is frankly hallucinatory. His controversies at home, where in 1299 Lull had obtained special permission to enter the synagogues and mosques to preach, never enjoyed the notoriety of the debates between Pau Cristía and Nachmanides. Always on the road, writing incessantly, usually on the crest of some high emotion, taking his missionary zeal over the seas or into Parisian lecture halls, Ramón the Fantastic exits from life a presumptive martyr. It was the death he ardently desired.

It is really incredible that this whirlwind of energy was able to produce works on spirituality which, if not of the highest order viewed from the vantage point of Teresa and John of the Cross, certainly do reflect intense piety, familiarity with the contemplative life, and refer directly to mystical phenomena. Two small works, the *Llibre de Amic et Amat* (Book of the Lover and the Beloved) and the *Art de Contemplació* (Art of Contemplation), both incorporated into his monumental allegorical novel, *Blanquerna*, are of unique interest to the historian of Christian spirituality. The host work, *Blanquerna,* is noteworthy in its own right. Some years ago, Allison Peers noted that "we do it less than justice if we fail to realize how little of the prose fiction in Europe is anterior to it."[15] Rightly so, as it is a century older than Froissart's *Chronicles*, Chaucer's *Canterbury Tales,* and Wycliffe's translation of the Bible, almost contemporary with Dante, prior to Boccaccio and Petrarch. Incongruously, it was a favorite of both Philip II of Spain and of the men of the eighteenth century enlightenment.

Blanquerna

A very brief resume of this voluminous work may serve as a sketchy introduction to Lull's treatises on spirituality. The first section of *Blanquerna* deals with episodes in the life of Blanquerna's parents who, when he leaves to live the life of a hermit, retire to a hospital to minister to the sick. It continues with a lengthy description of his quondam fiancee's life in a convent where eventually she is appointed Abbess. Blanquerna himself retires to a typically romantic Lullian forest, an idyllic pastoral scene in the shadow of a noble palace, and there meets ten ancients who represent the Ten Commandments,[16] who are engaged in lamenting the sad state of mankind. A nice touch is given by the Third Commandment who deplores that the "blasphemous Jews" honor the Sabbath with more fervor than the Christians honor Sunday.[17] The narrative, at this point, is lively, a pleasant change from the dreary minutiae concerning Natana's convent. The Commandments urge Blanquerna to endeavor to promote devotion and compunction in great prelates, princes, and religious, so that they—the Commandments—will be honored.[18] Blessed by each of the ten, Blanquerna moves on.

Meeting two noble ladies, Faith and Charity, who are accompanied by their elder brother, Understanding, he moves on to the palace of Lady Valor, the Lullian counterpart of St. Francis' Lady Poverty. Valor is the distillate of all the virtues: truth, liberality, courtesy, humility, loyalty, piety, gratitude, and knowledge are placed under this heading.[19] Blanquerna reaches the palace with two companions: a jester (a figure usually used to represent Ramón himself) and an emperor, but only he is permitted to enter. A tender scene follows in which he consoles Lady Valor, assuring her that God is omnipotent and the entire universe his creation. God himself will intervene to fulfill and perfect it. Valor will recover its proper status and be honored as she should be.[20]

After many adventures, Blanquerna enters a monastery and rises to the office of Abbot. After a hiatus marked by the delightful *Book of Ave Maria*, in which each chapter illustrates an event of his abbatial rule through a clause of the Hail Mary, he is consecrated Bishop. He then proceeds to reform his diocese in accordance with the letters of the Eight Beatitudes. Ultimately elected Pope, Blanquerna accepts responsibility for the sanctification and conversion of the world.[21] In this enterprise, he divides the world into twelve districts under the direction of Cardinals named after a clause of the *Gloria*. The scenario is frankly utopian. Cardinal *Laudamus te* and his agents are charged with praising God, while Cardinal *Benedicimus te* goes throughout the world blessing the different lands. Cardinal *In terra pax hominibus bonae voluntatis* is charged with inquiring whether men are at odds and then attempting to reconcile them. His first charge concerns a

Christian and a Jew who are continuously squabbling about religion. The Cardinal uses the Lullian Art to end the contention. The enemies are reconciled and continue their dialogue in friendship. Lull insists that as the human voice rises to song through the art of music, understanding rises to knowledge through his Art. The *Abbreviated Art* is cited.[22]

Blanquerna takes the name of *Gloria in excelsis Deo* and proceeds to address the Cardinals, pleading with them:

> ...to aid him in his task of giving glory to God in such a way that people can themselves restore the intention by which all offices and sciences exist and give glory to God, since the world had come to such a grievous pass that there is hardly anyone who has the proper relation to the end for which he was created nor for the office in which he is placed.[23]

This enterprise is furthered by decreeing that erudite religious be assigned to study various languages and sciences, and that houses of study in the pattern of Miramar be established throughout the world.[24] Among the additional projects, which would today be considered hardly ecumenical in temper, is the selection of a group of Moslems and Jews who are living in Christian nations and oblige them to learn Latin and study the Scriptures. Lull seems to have believed that this force-feeding would incline at least some of the group to convert and that these, in turn, would be instrumental in converting their brethren.[25] On a purely military level, Blanquerna advocates the union of the two great Orders of warrior-monks, the Knights Hospitallers and the Templars. They would also be taught the Art—to be precise the *Abbreviated Art*—which would enable them to better fulfill their task of defending the faith and acting as counsellors to men of importance. Expectedly, a major factor of this reform involves a concerted attempt to reduce all languages to one, a universal language which would create a common bond between peoples, standardize customs, and bring about mutual regard.[26]

Lull is giving literary expression to his desire to mend the world. The human world and the human beings which comprise it, the earthly hierarchies and their corresponding callings or offices, are not what they should be. They fail to reflect the purpose for which they were created. The gap between their *de facto* and their ontological status—between the objective structure of creation and the muddled efforts of humanity to reproduce it—has created a topsy-turvy world in which Lady Valor is dishonored. Lull's goal is to right the world, set it on a firm foundation, and his principal tool in this effort is his Art, the God-given method by which chaos is reduced to order. This Art he applies with almost obsessional, at times even ludicrous, single-mindedness. The elevation of Blanquerna from a simple monk to the Pontificate is the device by which Lull attempts to provide the different religious offices with a living exemplar of what they should be and a standard to be measured against. The reforms proposed in the *Blanquerna* are meant to restore the original meaning of each office and to erase the disfiguring accretions which have been added through sin, ignorance, and neglect.

Once human nature is restored to the state which was intended for it by God and corresponds to its exemplar in the Divine Mind, the transformation will be reflected by the unity of language, custom, law, and religion. It must be admitted, nevertheless, that when Blanquerna, as Pope, proposes the reduction of all languages to a single one, ostensibly for the sake of peace, it is very much a *pax romana*. His allocution to the Cardinals ends with an expression of hope that this work will help preachers to exercise their ministry among the infidel with increased efficacy so that "by this means... error will be more easily destroyed and the erring converted to the truth."[27] Moreover, even his proposal for the establishment of a sort of international grievance court to promote peace and concord among peoples[28] is only another means to the great end of reform, the conversion of the non-Christian world and the establishment of a universal Christian *respublica*. Lull believed that the Christian possessed a privileged insight into the created order, a privilege denied to his "pagan" contemporaries. Because of this the very process by which things are set right according to their divine purpose is simultaneously a process of conversion. This is precisely why the Art, which in Lull's view extends into life surpassing the properly logical domain, is such an extraordinary gift. It is a universal panacea, the beneficent effects of which will overflow into all areas of human activity.

The preceding comments can serve to explain the contrasting views regarding Ramón Lull's attitude towards non-Christians. On the one hand, his work is viewed as a medieval highpoint of positive relations between the faiths inviting cordial and respectful dialogue. On the other, as its nadir, it opens the door to the woeful abuses of the following centuries. It cannot be denied that Lull expresses admiration for the noble characteristics of Islam and Judaism, praises many of their customs, their sincerity in devotion, and seems to be truly sympathetic to their plight. But it must be understood that, in Lull's opinion, their plight is estrangement from Christianity. Because of this, Lull, as the self-styled "procurator to the infidel," finds himself conscience-bound to commend all possible measures which are directed towards effecting their conversion. In spite of the respectful hearing which their doctrines are given in his works and the responsive, even friendly attitude which he practiced and recommended, the goal is still conversion. During the last decade of his life, Lull's attitude hardened and he began thinking in terms of a new crusade and the application of additional practical sanctions.

Nonetheless, it is probably erroneous to interpret his approach as merely a ploy recommended to missionaries so that they could deceive their potential clients. Although Lull was far from ecumenical, at least according to present day standards, his concern for non-Christians seems to be genuine, at times even touching. Moreover, if, as stated previously, conversion entails more than a mere transfer from one set of beliefs to another—a righting of the person which puts him in conformity with the model of humanity in the Divine Mind—he could scarcely recommend a different approach. In this way, he is attempting to correct the defective copy in accordance with the model of the original. At the very end of *Blanquerna*, the Emperor, who is reintroduced at this point, chats with a Bishop on his way to the Roman Court. The Bishop informs him that he proposes to teach the *Abbreviated Art* there, and to petition the Pontiff, no longer Blanquerna, to have it taught at all houses of general studies. He insists that this measure should effectively increase both devotion and understanding and take the knowledge of God to the "infidel." Precise thinking leads directly to increased devotion.[29]

The Book of the Lover and the Beloved
The Art of Contemplation

The two works in which Lull's spirituality is best and most clearly presented are the *Book of the Lover and the Beloved* and the *Art of Contemplation,* both of which are incorporated into the *Blanquerna.* When Pope Blanquerna resigns from the papacy to dedicate himself to the contemplative life—whether this was written before the "gran rifuto" of Pope Celestine V has been much debated—he is asked to provide a group of monks with an Art which will enable them to contemplate in the proper manner.[30] The narrative continues with Blanquerna acceding to their wishes, giving himself up to fervent prayer asking God to provide him with the solution. This prayer elevates the "powers" of his soul to their "highest degree." Because of its fervor and devotion the soul is drawn "outside" of itself. Blanquerna comes to the realization that love does not follow a predetermined method when the Lover loves the Beloved,[31] that the act of contemplation always transcends the method which prepares the way for it. He admits that he is emulating the holy men of Islam who, by means of brief sayings, produce such intense devotion that the understanding is prodded to ascend ever higher in contemplation.[32]

But this is not an outright rejection of method. In the *Art of Contemplation* method has not been rejected but merely placed in a subordinate position. A good illustration of this is that any attempt to organize the 360 or so sayings found in the *Book of the Lover and the Beloved* has to be done in tandem with the *Art of Contemplation.* To translate them precisely into traditional mystical categories is simply impossible. This means that any interpretation will be somewhat arbitrary though even an arbitrary interpretation carries some weight when placed within the exigencies of the Art.

The monks requested an Art which would enable them to rise to the contemplation of God. Lull responds with an intricate, quasi-mathematical method which calls into play an entire spectrum of possibilities. Divided into twelve parts the method endeavors to contemplate the divine attributes through multiple viewpoints and by means of combinations and permutations. His goal is to effectively etch these attributes on the three "faculties" of the soul: memory, understanding, and will.[33]

This spiritual adaptation of the *ars combinatoria* is not a merely mechanical process but requires certain preconditions for its use. Lull suggests that the person must be in a disposition favorable to contemplation, residing in a convenient and suitable place. Circumstances such as psychological hindrances—he mentions a tendency to exaggerate reflection or affect—and even external stimuli such as excessive noise, heat, or cold, are able to stall the process. The principal requisite, a traditional staple of the contemplative life, is detachment from the care of temporal things in memory, understanding, and will.[34] Denis' *aphairesis*, or a pragmatic version thereof, has here been demoted to playing a preparatory role. There is no longer a radical ascent through negations which, applied with uncompromising logic, leads to mystical contemplation. The level of speculation has doubtless suffered as a consequence.

The first chapter of the *Art of Contemplation* gives an appropriately idyllic picture of Blanquerna's method of prayer. Rising at midnight, he views the heavens while discarding all "worldly things" from his consideration and begins to meditate on the Divine Goodness. First, he meditates on this attribute as it is found intermingled with the other divine perfections (Lull mentions sixteen), and then as each of these perfections are found in Divine Goodness. He kneels and "lifts his hands up to heaven and his thoughts to God," says an appropriate prayer, and then meditates on the preceding skein of thoughts with all the powers of his soul.[35] The very power by which the Sovereign Good is invoked elevates his meditation "above the firmament" to that Great Good, which Lull compares to a lightning bolt having six dimensions (high, low, right, left, in front of, in back of), infinite movement, and in possession of eternity.[36]

Although this image is somewhat curious even for Ramón Lull, it refers to a model of Christian spirituality which should be familiar by now. An initial demand for moral and spiritual purification is followed by meditation in which the object of contemplation, in this case the Divine Goodness, is in some way apprehended. Lull adds a novel turn: meditation, as he describes it, is the work of both imagination and reason. These are under the direction of the Art which generates increased devotion, and in turn elevates the soul to a transcendent reality which can be expressed only through symbol and metaphor.[37]

As indicated, Lull's spirituality has both intellectual and affective aspects. He notes that when persevering in meditation his heart begins to "catch fire" and his eyes to water, due to the intense emotions he experiences in remembering, understanding, and loving the divine perfections. It is noteworthy that he gives the gift of tears a privileged status, as it seems to act as a somatic verification of elevated contemplation. But all is not a smooth upward movement. In his account, prior to "weeping perfectly" an abrupt downward movement occurs which is produced by the understanding falling to the level of the imagination. Tears cease and doubt begins to surface. How is it possible for God to possess these perfections prior to creation? Other questions rise to the surface.

But this rising flood of doubt has an antidote. Lull advises that it is necessary to detach the understanding from the imagination by remembering that as the Supreme Good is infinite in perfection, it must possess all attributes in a perfect manner.[38] This thought "inflames" his heart and his eyes fill with copious tears.[39] Following in the rationalistic tradition, Lull mistrusts the imagination and holds it in low esteem, an attitude common to classical Greek thought and found in many later mystical writers including Teresa of Avila and John of the Cross. It is later echoed in the so-called Continental Rationalism of the sixteenth and seventeenth centuries. Not very far removed from Freud's notion of *mentation*—thinking in pictures which is common to psychotics, children, and the dream world—the imagination has the capacity to bring about irregular, shall we say freelance, combinations of images which degrades the intellect and undermines contemplation. The strict, systematic, computer-like combinations of Lull's Art counters this movement of the imagination to structure the noetic aspect of contemplation. It increases devotion and prods the understanding to move higher.

Lull never ceases to surprise. He goes so far as to personify the "faculties" of the soul (memory, understanding, and will) and has them enter into dialogue regarding the divine perfections. Yet, even these novel personages are subject to the Art in their deliberations moving rigorously from memory, to understanding, to will.[40] The Art does not produce contemplation. It merely engenders in the soul a sort of receptivity to the free action of God. Because of this, Blanquerna prefaces his own contemplation of the Trinity with a prayer which asks God to elevate the powers of his soul so that he may ascend to contemplation.[41]

But the Art certainly does cooperate with grace. Lull provides a pithy but clear example of his method of prayer. He first affirms a divine perfection—"God is good"—and then proceeds to deny this very same perfection—"God is not good because of the evil in the world." The affirmation is finally reinstated after the loss of devotion and knowledge caused by this denial is surpassed. It brings in its wake an increase of love and knowledge in contemplation.[42] Although this method does include affirmative and negative moments it really has little resemblance to the affirmative and negative "theologies" of Denis or, for that matter, to the conflation of both proposed by Bonaventure and Thomas Aquinas. In Lull the divine humanity of Christ becomes a proper object of contemplation, and both the divine initiative and the role of love is stressed. The *Book of Contemplation* ends with a prayer which indicates the ineffable character of Blanquerna's contemplation. Only God, "his teacher," is able to comprehend it.[43]

The aphorisms and epigrams of *The Book of the Lover and the Beloved* are not intended to replace the Art but to use it as the point of departure in order to stimulate the soul to devotion. It was ostensibly written by Blanquerna after having contemplated God and his attributes with the purpose of enabling the soul to meditate within a short period of time.[44] Emulating the Sufies of Islam, these "sayings" intended to enkindle devotion, stimulate understanding, and impel the soul to ascend to higher levels of contemplation. These "sayings" include aphorisms, epigrams, exclamations, narratives, puzzles, questions, and parables, in which the inhabitants of the heavenly court rub elbows with the motley thirteenth century Levantine world and the denizens of Ramón's fertile imagination. Love chats with Fear and Hope. Birds sing of the highest realities. The protagonists are the

Lover (*Amic*) and the Beloved (*Amat*), which is to say, the human soul and God, encountered as Christ, Trinity, and Godhead.

Whatever the novelty of Lull's spirituality, there is the ever-present temptation of forcing the sayings of the *Llibre de Amic e Amat* into the traditional Procrustean bed of purgative, illuminative, and unitive. And fall we must as there are few if any working categories available! But it should be understood as providing general lines for interpretation and no more. In addition, the Sufi influence on Lull cannot be determined with precision and this adds to the difficulty of the task. It is known that a type of "contemplation" induced by the repeated recitation of ejaculations meant to bring God to mind was current in Islamic circles at the time. These sayings were meant to evoke responses such as humility and shame in the presence of God, purity of intention in serving him, desire to practice austerity, and so forth. As early as the eleventh century, Algazel recommends that the spirit of "affective effusion" should accompany liturgical prayer and that pious readings be accompanied by an affective response and practical resolutions.[45] Indeed, methodical meditation had its origin in Islam where the role played by the affects was emphasized. In this light, perhaps Lull could be viewed as a forerunner of Ignatius of Loyola and the *Spiritual Exercises.*

Some of the most forceful sayings in the *Llibre de Amic e Amat* concern the Lover's vocation. His task is to restore purpose in the world: "When will water, accustomed to flow downhill, take on the nature of ascending"; "when will the innocent outnumber the guilty."[46] Mankind follows the descending current, committing the most heinous offenses which Lull never tires of lamenting: despising the Beloved.[47] Christ, who came to earth to honor mankind is dishonored by man.[48] The Lover searches frenetically for true devotion to the Beloved, "through plains and mountain tops," and returns in frank disillusion.[49] The "infidel" is lost to the Beloved through ignorance alone.[50] In an authentically moving passage, Lull deplores the death of a man who died without love: no one had taught him the Art of love.[51]

Lull's outrage generated a multiplicity of schemes directed to correct this injustice. The missionary effort is only the preliminary move of a universal enterprise of reform which would eventually turn inward to transform a tepid Christianity. He was convinced that lack of virtue was the root cause of the many troubles which plague humanity. This is evidenced by his defense of chivalry, a calling which has the goal of knowing, honoring, serving, and fearing God.[52] Lull was convinced that after the Fall the virtues—and justice is the social virtue *par excellence*—are able to inspire respect through fear alone. Thus the need for *Realpolitik*. Ramón's imagination rises to the occasion. From each thousand men the most virtuous was chosen for this office. Attached to his person is the most beautiful of animals, the horse, and the most noble of weapons.[53] The role of the knight is ancillary to that of the priest. While the clergy instills love of God and devotion to him, the knight instills the salutary fear which is necessary for the maintenance of the social order. Only in this way can men be dissuaded from harming each other. It is evident that Lull makes knighthood into an Art, a science which is capable of demonstration and can be taught.[54]

The principal task of the knight's calling is then to uphold Christianity, complementing the missionary efforts of the clergy. When he wrote the *Book of the Order of Chivalry* (1275), some years before the elaboration of his ambitious crusading projects, Lull was already concerned with the present danger of a militant Islam, a concern which increased with time. Perhaps he thought of himself as the synthesis of the offices of cleric and knight. To the present day, Spanish traditionalist thought considers the clergy and military as the two least corruptible professions and the bulwarks against revolution.

Lull did not minimize the enormous difficulties involved in proselytization except perhaps in those rosy passages dealing with the Art. More representative is one of the sayings from the *Llibre de Amic e Amat*:

> Tell me Fool: What is a marvel? He answered that it is a marvel to love things absent more than things present, and love visible, corruptible things more than visible and incorruptible things.[55]

The spiritual life advocated by Lull is predicated on a frank austerity of life. His sometimes euphoric, usually emphatic language juxtaposes the delights and also the afflictions which arise in the Lover/Beloved relationship. The Lover is said to "sicken" because of the Beloved and is at times incapable of differentiating between torment and joy.[56] He stresses the need for solitude, detachment from things, and corporeal discipline,[57] but at times moves to less traditional grounds:

> The Lover forgot all below the high heaven so that the understanding could rise higher to know the Beloved, who the will aspired to praise and contemplate.[58]

It seems that the closer the Lover approaches the Beloved, the more torment; and the more torment, the more love.[59] Each elevation of the soul generates an increase of both torment and joy until the Beloved "heals" the soul.

This movement is described in metaphors which have become traditional. The "cloud" between the Lover and the Beloved, when illumined by love, becomes clear and luminous, the medium through which Lover and Beloved "speak" to each other.[60] Lull has the light from the Beloved's dwelling place illuminating the dwelling place of the Lover, casting out shadows and filling it with delight.[61] It leads to an elevation of the soul in which human speech is transcended and "sight" takes its place.[62] In the courtly language of the day, the Beloved is said to give himself in payment for the services of the Lover,[63] and to receive him at his court.[64] Both the aspect of union and that of separation are portrayed. In a text recalling the more convoluted passages of John of the Cross we find: "I will contemplate the contemplation of your contemplation by the contemplation of your contemplation."[65] And this is moderated by a saying which indicates that although Lover and Beloved are distinct things they are, after a manner, made one through love.[66]

Predictably, the most tender passages deal with love. The summons of love and hope, "*amb colp d'amor e esperança*," bids the Lover enter into the presence of the Beloved by passing through the doors of divinity and humanity.[67] It is a nice variation on the theme of Christ as the "door" which leads to deification, the "ladder" between man and God. This love is also compared to the mixture of wine and water, with Lull taking full advantage of the theological nuances involved.[68] The notion of *sobria ebrietas* (sober inebriation), a stock phrase of the literature of mysticism, is found in the "sayings" several times as is the mirror-image analogy.[69] Lover and Beloved are complementary images. God is the mirror in which man can acquire self-knowledge.[70]

These sayings point to a high order of spirituality. Mystical phenomena are mentioned albeit sparsely and, at times, obliquely. Ecstasy, tears, and swoonings are referred to as are experiences which are called "dyings" and "languishings."[71] The sober inebriation passages also fall into the category. There is even one passage which seems to refer to a mystical revelation of the Trinity.[72] Nonetheless, compared to the lengthy catalogs found in the writings of later mystical writers and the subsequent schematizations of the theologians, Ramón Lull, in this respect at least, is not particularly fantastic. On the contrary, he is somewhat on the sober side.

A further point. This zealous missionary was not at ease with a purely contemplative spirituality. Like Socrates' philosopher, he must return to the cave and decipher the shadows and echoes: "the secrets of my Beloved torment me when my works do not manifest them and my mouth keeps them secret by not revealing them to the people."[73] The contemplation of Mary should provide the momentum for the activity of Martha so as to renew and strengthen it. Ramón the Jester, the *Foll,* must be faithful to his calling of proclaiming the supreme worth of the Beloved. Lull insists that mystical favors are of special value when they inspire fidelity to one's trust, one's calling. One saying has the Lover ascending to the Beloved and contemplating him with delight but then being obliged to go down into the world to contemplate him in grief and tribulation.[74] Lull's vocation as "Procurator to the Infidel" is present even at the highest reaches of his flight. The highest contemplation should overflow into missionary activity.

No matter how blandly pious some of the sayings from the *Book of the Lover and the Beloved* may be, there are few lapses into the saccharine. Although much may strike us as naive and many passages could find their place in a handbook of religious truisms, Lull has the facility of adding a novel twist by use of a fortuitous metaphor or a surprising interpretation. His piety is always dogmatically grounded with the Art as its systematic watchdog. The Beloved is identified with Sovereign Good, Glory, Power, Wisdom, Love, Jesus Christ, and the Infinite Lover.[75] On the horizon where spirituality, theology, and philosophy merge, the Beloved is seen as bringing about a great transmutation of values, something in line with Nicholas of Cusa's coincidence of opposites.[76] In one of its most touching passages Lull gives a description of the Beloved's coat of arms. It bears a dead man: "He was a dead man crucified. Those who call themselves lovers will follow him."[77]

The Lover is called a fool, a madman, and a jester. As he is behaving like a madman the Lover is asked if he has lost his wits. He responds:

> The Beloved has stolen his will and was given his understanding so that he was left with memory alone, by which he remembered his Beloved.[78]

This is doubtless an excellent if pithy description of the higher stages of the mystical life. But the Lover still considers himself the Beloved's messenger to Christian and "Infidel" princes with the duty of teaching his Art to them so that they will know and love him.[79] Quite simply, self-perfection and the evangelization of the world go in tandem.

On the metaphysical level, the Lover moves towards being by means of the perfection of the Beloved and falls towards nothingness through his own deficiency.[80] This is a traditional Augustinian theme which finds perhaps its most ingenious reflection in Bonaventure's theory of *vertibilitas*. The move towards God is always a move towards being. Somewhat like the Platonic *eros*, Ramón's "love" occupies a position between Lover and Beloved but, unlike the movement given in the *Symposium*, here it brings about *both* an ascent of the Lover to the Beloved and the descent of the Beloved to the Lover. Lull also provides a superb answer to the question regarding God's activity prior to creation: "My Beloved loved."[81]

Although, as mentioned previously, the main goal of these sayings is to stimulate devotion—the very basis of the Christian spiritual life—the agreement of the human will with the divine, is also clearly stated:

> The Beloved said: Do you possess will? He answered that the servant and captive has no will other than to obey his Lord and Beloved.[82]

The will is "imprisoned" by the Beloved. Moreover, even his rather pedantic definition of love moves in the same direction: "love is the concordance of theory and practice in the will of the Lover which empowers him to inspire people to honor and serve his Beloved."[83] This agreement of the human and divine wills is the very ground of the life of perfection.

The free action of God on the human soul transfers it to a new dimension. Lull indicates that while "acquired science" is obtained through study and the work of the intellect, "infused science" is obtained through will, devotion, and prayer.[84] It becomes evident that these three (will, devotion, and prayer) are themselves not the cause of infused science but only the point of departure for divine grace. He repeatedly states that the *first principle* of love is found in the nobility of the Beloved who sows the seeds of virtue and love in the heart of the Lover.[85] The faith and devotion which comprise the "ladder" by which the soul is elevated to the understanding of "divine secrets" originates in the Beloved.[86]

Epilogue

Although Lull's imagery is exotic—at times so alien as to be disturbing—he is nevertheless following traditional paths. Saints Paul, Augustine, and Anselm are not far distant. It is scarcely mere chance that the Feast of the Conversion of St. Paul is the day commonly assigned to Lull's conversion. Popular folklore has it that on this day his cave on Mount Randa is filled with perfume.[87] Whatever the case, his spirituality impresses one as extremely intense in its fervor and unique in its practical orientation with the affective element reaching its height in the *Book of the Lover and the Beloved* which can reasonably be considered the work of an ecstatic after the manner of Jacopone da Todi. It certainly reflects an important aspect of his personality. This jester of God who wrote the hauntingly lovely *Plant de la Verge* (*Lament of the Virgin*), and the stately *Hores de Nostra Dona* (*Hours of Our Lady*), could occasionally reach poetic heights.

But Lull is plagued by overabundance. He can never leave well enough alone. He feels impelled to preach, to expound, to teach. His poems never reach the light and holy as do those of John of the Cross. At times they seem to be the expressions of a mind which has hardened into the ominous geometrical figures of the Art with their multiplicity of combinations and permutations. Ramón Lull was, in many ways, a disjointed man such as is often found in the history of Spain and which has its exemplar in the Don Quixote/Sancho Panza bifurcation. Courtier, jester, missionary, poet, fool, mystic, and computer, Lull belongs to this tradition. Although the affective part of his personality is allowed to roam it is always within the boundaries set by the Art. The Art is no less than the method by which life itself is increased and directed to its proper end in God. It increases devotion by multiplying the possible objects of meditation, enriches life by expanding its possibilities, and serves to structure thought.

Lull has gained more recognition through his Art than his literary works. His favorite projects came to a sad end, and even his memory was subjected to a vicious persecution by the Dominican Inquisitor, Nicholas Eymeric, who believed that his works contained no less than five hundred errors. But there were better days to come. In the fifteenth century a Lullian school was established at Barcelona and his thought introduced into the University of Alcalá by Cardinal Cisneros in the sixteenth century. At the Council of Trent his teachings were declared orthodox. Moreover, an unverified tradition has Pope Leo X proclaiming his beatification. The eighteenth century provided a serious defense of Lull and a severe repudiation of his critics in the *Vindiciae Lullianae* written by the Cistercian, Ramón Pasqual.

Nicholas of Cusa and Leibniz were among the many notables to be impressed and inspired by the Art. Strange to say, in Leibniz's day many of the most renowned philosophers were regarded as "Lullists," and this included Gassendi, Giordano Bruno, and Hobbes.[88] In his *De parte combinatoria*, Leibniz refers to individual works of Lull as well as to commentaries on them.[89] He was himself concerned with combinatorial methods from the age of twelve or thirteen and for no little period infatuated with its possibilities. A letter of October, 1671, to Duke Johann Friedrich, expresses his enthusiasm:

> In philosophy I have discovered a method of achieving in all sciences by means of the *ars combinatoria* what Descartes and others have achieved in arithmetic and geometry by algebra and analysis. The *ars* was first developed by Lull and P. Kircher but they were far from recognizing all its

potentialities. By its means all notions in the world can be reduced to a few simple terms which serve as an alphabet and by using combinations of this alphabet a means will be found to discover systematically all things together with their theorems and whatever can be found out about them. This invention. . . is considered by me to be the mother of all inventions and to be the most important of all even though it may not be recognized as such at the moment.[90]

This is, to be sure, a very clear presentation of the substance of Lull's Art. Leibniz's view of his limited vision regarding the Art's possibilities may well be one of the great ironies of intellectual history.

Ramón Lull remains an enigmatic, not to say elusive, figure. At one time it was thought that he had written well over a thousand works. He did write from 150 to 200,[91] still an impressive figure. The former figure would have been truly incredible. But this dovetails, after a fashion, with the accounts of his beatification, probably apocryphal, and of his death as a martyr, rather too good to be true. His many travels titillate more than inform, and his missionary efforts melt into the general cacophony of the age. He comes after the Crusades and before the Black Death. Even the most famous anecdote concerning the man stems from a probable visit and an improbable encounter but nevertheless carries the heady fragrance of the Blessed Ramón. We find him, aged and hoary bearded, sitting at the feet of Duns Scotus at Paris. Seeing the bizarre old man who is following his lecture and reacting to the points being made, Duns Scotus asks him a simple grammatical question: "Dominus, quae pars?" (Lord is what part of speech?). Ramón replies: "Dominus non est pars, sed totua" (The Lord is not a part but the whole).[92] Whether apocryphal or not, the story illustrates Lull's pyrotechnic intelligence which is found in his works, where dulling excess is lightened by passages of surprising insight and even beauty.

His contributions to literature, philosophy, logic, and spirituality were certainly extensive. It was due largely to Lull that Catalan preceded other European languages as a vehicle for philosophy and poetry. His *Blanquerna* affords him a privileged role in the early history of the novel. His Art led, as we have seen, to Liebniz's *ars combinatoria,* which can be considered as related to the ancient quest for the *lingua adamica,* the original, unitary language of mankind. Insofar as spirituality is concerned, he presents a technically novel but nevertheless traditional account of the Christian spiritual life. The Dionysian residue, though modified in the tradition of the Victorines and Bonaventure, is still present to some degree.

Lull's spirituality is distinguished by its exotic packaging, its richness and prolixity, and the use made of the Art. Poetry, allegory, borrowings from *chansons de geste,* Islamic affective techniques, perhaps even scrapings from the *Kabbalah,* are all indiscriminately placed under its tutelage. He quite naturally and insistently juxtaposes his Art, the founding of language schools, missionary work, and the aspiration for martyrdom. Even his frenetic and erratic missionary work was not without structure. The Art can be applied to any human activity so as to structure it and in so doing lead the soul to God. That Ramón Lull was imprudent, often bellicose, rarely measured, and never predictable, adds to the romance. The heights of his own spiritual life, as with all mystics, was hidden from public view. In a decadent age, much like our own, he aspired to better things, to a dramatic renewal of mankind. In the words by which the Emperor of *Blanquerna* charged the Jester of Valor to sing at the Papal Court:

Nada és novella frevós
e renòvellen li desir
del apòstols, qui lausant vos
anaven mort, plaent sentir.

Notes

[1] Refer to the excellent study of Jeremy Cohen, *The Friars and the Jews: The Evolution of Medieval Anti-Judaism,* (Ithaca: Cornell University Press, 1982). Also Amos Funkenstein, "Changes in the Patterns of Christian Anti-Jewish Polemic in the Twelfth Century" [Hebrew], *Zion,* n.s. 33 (1968).

[2] *Ibid.,* Chapter 3, "The Attack on Rabbinic Literature," pp. 51-76. Also Edward A. Synan, *The Popes and Jews in the Middle Ages,* (New York: Macmillan, 1915).

[3] *In Ioannis Evangelium,* 11, 8; *Epistola* 149, 9; *Sermo* 201, 3; *De Fide Rerum Quae Non Videtur* 6, 9. Refer to the Latin/Spanish bilingual edition, *Obras de San Agustín,* under the direction of Felix García, 18 vols., (Madrid: BAC, 1957-1959).

[4] *De fide rerum, loc. cit.*

[5] By J. Cohen, *op. cit.,* pp. 242-264.

[6] *Ibid.,* p. 54, citing Joseph Shatzmiller, "Towards a Picture of the First Maimonidean Controversy" [Hebrew], *Zion,* n.s. 34 (1969), pp. 126-144.

[7] *Ibid.,* p. 199. Salo Baron credits Lull with being the "Leader" of the Council of Vienne which adopted strict canons against usury. Salo D. Baron, *A Social and Religious History of the Jews,* vol. XII, (New York: Columbia University Press, 1967), p. 157; also pp. 134-154.

[8] Literary works are found in *Obres Essencials,* 2 vols., 1957-1960. Refer to *Ramón Lull, Obras Literarias,* notes by M. Batllori and M. Caldentey, (Madrid: BAC, 1948). Also E. Allison Peers, *Ramón Lull: A Biography* [reprint], (New York: B. Franklin, 1969); Armand Llinares, *Raymond Lull: philosophie de l'action,* (Paris: PUF, 1963); J. N. Hilgarth, *Ramon Lull and Lullism in Fourteenth Century France,* (New York: O.U.P., 1971).

[9] *Vida coetania,* 2. A Latin/Catalan text in *Obras Literarias,* pp. 43-78.

[10] *Ibid.,* 3.

[11] *Desconhort,* II. A Spanish/Catalan text in *Obras Literarias,* pp. 1094-1147.

[12] E. Allison Peers, *op. cit.,* p. 84ff.

[13] *Vida coetania,* 14.

[14] *Desconhort,* viii; xxxviiiff.

[15] Allison Peers, *op. cit.,* p. 167ff.

[16] *Blanquerna,* 42, 2. A Spanish translation is given in *Obras Literarias,* pp. 159-596.

[17] *Ibid.,* 42, 8.

[18] *Ibid.,* 42, 16.

[19] *Ibid.,* 48, 3.

[20] *Ibid.,* 48, 10.

[21] *Ibid.,* 79, 9.

[22] *Ibid.,* 81, 4.

[23] *Ibid.,* 80, 1.

[24] *Ibid.,* 80, 3.

[25] *Ibid.,* 80, 5.

[26] *Ibid.,* 94, 6.

[27] *Idem.*

[28] *Ibid.,* 95, 5.

[29]*Art de Contemplació*, XIV, 3. This book is incorporated into *Blanquerna* as its final chapter.

[30]*Blanquerna*, 96, 3; 98, 2.

[31]*Ibid.*, 99, 2.

[32]*Ibid.*, 99, 3.

[33]*Art de Contemplació*, Prol., 3-4.

[34]*Ibid.*, Prol. 5.

[35]*Ibid.*, I, 1.

[36]*Ibid.*, I, 4.

[37]*Idem.*

[38]*Ibid.*, I, 4-5.

[39]*Ibid.*, I, 6.

[40]*Ibid.*, I, 7-8.

[41]*Ibid.*, V, 1.

[42]*Ibid.*, V, 3.

[43]*Ibid.*, XIII, 7.

[44]*Llibre de Amic e Amat*, Prol. 1. This book is incorporated into *Blanquerna* as its chapter 99.

[45]Somewhat ancient but still informative is Miguel Asin Palacios, *El Islam Cristianizado*, (Madrid: Plutarco, 1931), p. 176ff.

[46]*Llibre de Amic e Amat*, 4.

[47]*Ibid.*, 253.

[48]*Ibid.*, 99; 127; 128.

[49]*Ibid.*, 34.

[50]*Ibid.*, 263.

[51]*Ibid.*, 209.

[52]*Llibre del Orde de Cavalleria* I, 1. A Spanish translation is given in *Obras Literarias*, pp. 105-141.

[53]*Ibid.*, I, 2-4.

[54]*Ibid.*, I, 14.

[55]*Llibre de Amic e Amat*, 84.

[56]*Ibid.*, 5; 8.

[57]*Ibid.*, 46; 137; 234.

[58]*Ibid.*, 139.

[59]*Ibid.*, 244.

[60]*Ibid.*, 123.

[61]*Ibid.*, 100.

[62]*Ibid.*, 27; 152.

[63]*Ibid.*, 64.

[64]*Ibid.*, 96.

[65]*Ibid.*, 257.

[66]*Ibid.*, 211.

[67]*Ibid.*, 43.

[68]*Ibid.*, 50.

[69]*Ibid.*, 283; 284; 364.

[70]*Ibid.*, 350.

[71]*Ibid.*, 89; 168.

[72]*Ibid.*, 269.

[73]*Ibid.*, 32.

[74]*Ibid.*, 56.

[75]*Ibid.*, 37.

[76]*Ibid.*, 279; 338.

[77]*Ibid.*, 101.

[78]*Ibid.*, 54.

[79]*Ibid.*, 143.

[80]*Ibid.*, 315.

[81]*Ibid.*, 258; 263.

[82]*Ibid.*, 220.

[83]*Ibid.*, 236.

[84]*Ibid.*, 241.

[85]*Ibid.*, 61; 94.

[86]*Ibid.*, 288.

[87]Allison Peers., *op. cit.*, p. 106.

[88]Refer to Gottfried Martin, *Leibniz: Logic and Metaphysics*, trans. by R. J. Northcott and P. Lucas, (Manchester: Manchester University Press, 1964), p. 24ff.

[89]Cited in *op. cit.*, p. 24.

[90]Found in *Die philosophischen Schriften von G. W. Leibniz*, ed. G. I. Gerhardt, (Berlin), 1875ff., vol. I, 57.

[91]Refer to Ephrem Longpré, "Lulle (Raymond)," *Dictionnaire de Théologie Catholique*, vol. IX, 1926, col. 1072-1141.

[92]Cited by Allison Peers, *op, cit.*, p. 323.

IV
Teresa of Avila

Entering the Court of the Kings in the vast, impressive hulk that is the Monastery of San Lorenzo del Escorial, the traveler is greeted by the imposing figures of six Old Testament kings: David, Solomon, Hezekiah, Josiah, Josaphat, and Manasseh. The inscriptions in Latin indicate that David received the model of the Temple from God, that Solomon dedicated it, Hezekiah restored it, and Manasseh rebuilt the altar. It goes on to indicate that Josiah recovered the Book of the Law and Josaphat disseminated its legislation. Philip II spent no little time and care overseeing the construction of this Monastery-Palace. With his customary officiousness, he supervised even the smallest detail. The monarch took the symbolism quite seriously. Spain was the new Israel charged by the Almighty to preserve his law and extend his domain even to those far corners of the globe in which Philip's intrepid armies and no less intrepid missionaries were testing their mettle. Conquest was in the air, conquest which was both horizontal and vertical. The age is summarized by the title of a work by the Franciscan mystic, Fray Juan de los Angeles, *Diálogos de la Conquista del reino de Dios* (*Dialogues of the Conquest of the Kingdom of God*).

The monastery gives mute testimony to Philip's history, personality, and temperament. It was built in thanksgiving for the Spanish victory over the French at St. Quentin (August 10, 1557), and was completed in September, 1584, when Spanish fortunes were not as sanguine. A few years later, Philip received the crushing news of the defeat of the *Invencible* (The Armada) while praying in the chapel. After his reign, the Monastery was gradually replaced as a major royal residence, and the gigantic, ornate, Palacio de Oriente was built in Madrid. In the Escorial, the small room in which Philip II received Ambassadors and the painfully smaller room in which he slept are in stark contrast to the vastness of the edifice with its 88 fountains, 1,200 doors, and 2,663 windows. With typical Spanish disregard for specialization, the edifice houses a palace, a monastery, and the royal pantheon, as if the totality of human existence could be comprised within its walls.

Like its royal benefactor, the monastery of San Lorenzo has elicited mixed reactions. Some believe that the building is an architectural marvel while others condemn it as totally lacking in aesthetic value. Menendez y Pelayo—that quintessential Spanish Catholic—viewed Philip as unsympathetic, dry, and prosaic but tenacious and persistent, lacking brilliance but usually sincere and scarcely an opportunist. In spite of Philip's reputation as an obscurantist, Menendez Pelayo indicates that his contributions to human culture were quite extensive.[1] San Lorenzo can be said to mirror these royal character traits. The man who preferred the grotesqueries of Hieronymus Bosch to the Byzantine splendors of El Greco guided the hand of its architect with rarely equalled persistence. Perhaps because of this Menendez Pelayo can speak of the "freezing breath" of Herrera's architecture: pure, austere, and cold. Geometric beauty without grace, grandeur without warmth.[2]

Notwithstanding, San Lorenzo del Escorial is a fitting monument to a race of ambivalence and virile will, perhaps all too ready to dominate and mold sinful humanity. Herrera, its architect, was a mathematician and an ardent follower of Ramón Lull's Art.[3] But no matter how geometrically frigid the architecture, the society which swarmed around it reflected the duality of the monarch to a greater extent than his austere foundation. The violence of the warrior was more than matched by the self-violence of the ascetic; the impetuousness of the libertine rivaled the zeal of the monk and friar. Extremes of corruption and sanctity existed side by side. The reformation of religious orders proceeded apace with the bizarre excesses of the *alumbrados*. The very same Inquistion which "relaxed" heretics established academies for the study of mathematics. The greatest literary work of the age would be penned by Cervantes in a valiant attempt to portray the tidal oscillations between sense and spirit, the practical and the ideal, which characterized its spirit.

Background

Teresa was a middle-aged nun of about forty-two years of age when the battle of St. Quentin was fought. At about this time she experienced her first visions and locutions. John of the Cross was a young lad working in a hospital at Toledo. By the time the Escorial was completed, Teresa had died at Alba de Tormes on October 4, 1582, a physical wreck and a spiritual giant, the foundress of an Order which was burgeoning rapidly. John of the Cross was completing the first redaction of the *Cántico Espiritual.* Eight years later he died at Ubeda after having been deprived of his office and maltreated physically and morally. The charming, naive, Fray Gracian de la Madre de Dios, Teresa's friend and first Provincial of the Discalced, was expelled from the Order. His opponent, Nicholas Doria, was appointed the first Discalced Carmelite General. On May 9, 1594, less than six months later, he also died. The Order continued to flourish.[4]

The startling contrasts of the *Siglo de Oro* with its milling nobility and peasantry, sobersides and *picaros,* priests, students, monks, and visionaries, provided the texture of Teresa's world albeit her own life, at least before she began her foundations, was the quiet, commonplace life of a nun living in a none too severe convent. The only noteworthy fact concerns her ancestry. Her grandfather, Don Juan Sanchez, was a converted Jew and Judaizer, who confessed and was pardoned, receiving a penance of wearing a *sanbenito* (penitential garment) for seven weeks during the Friday procession of those persons reconciled to the Church.[5] His children were also reconciled with the exception of the eldest son, Hernando, who studied at Salamanca and probably died at a relatively young age. In any case, Don Juan Sanchez moved from Toledo to Avila, probably in the pursuit of a welcome anonymity, settled there, and his sons were able to make advantageous marriages. One of these sons, Don Alonso, married twice. His second wife was Doña Beatriz de Ahumada, who bore him several children, one of whom was Teresa.

Apart from the minor world of family and the major world of history, another domain would prove to be of great importance in the life of Teresa, that of spirituality. Even today we are surprised at the good taste and discretion which she showed in her spiritual readings. Although hardly an educated woman, and harboring a lifelong distaste for *bachilleras* (lettered women), she was nevertheless engulfed in a spiritual movement which had been buffeting Iberia for some time. The spirituality of sixteenth century Spain was, to a considerable extent, derived from the *devotio moderna*[6] which pressed the importance of the subjective and affective in the religious life. It became systematized with devotion leading to conversion, interior prayer, and contemplation. It was Gerard Groot who led a reaction against speculative mysticism and the monastic liturgy. The Brethren of the Common Life intervened effectively in the religious life of the day to prod many members of the established orders, both monastic and mendicant, to a more intense spiritual life.

The last great work of this spiritual age, John Mauburnus' *Rosetum*, influenced the thought of Francisco de Osuna whose *Tercer Abecedario* produced a very favorable reaction in Teresa. The most famous work, *The Imitation of Christ*, became normative reading matter for all pious Spaniards. Its effect was substantial and probably linked to increasing anti-intellectualism. Ignatius of Loyola, for example, praised the *Imitation* highly and attacked the pallid intellectualism of Erasmus with evident aversion. Today this smallish tome is used, when at all, as a devotional tract, a book of spiritual readings, which probably strikes the contemporary reader as florid, affected, and remote. Its author, Thomas à Kempis, composed an affect-oriented meditation on the humanity of Christ which is intended to lead to ultimate union with God. It was enormously successful.

Teresa read Augustine—she repeatedly recalls her emotions on reading the *Confessions*—Gregory the Great and two Spaniards: the Abbot of Montserrat, Garcia de Cisneros, and the ecstatic Franciscan lay brother, Bernardino de Laredo, who in 1535 published a treatise on contemplative prayer, the *Subida del Monte Sion* in which the Dionysian imprint is clearly visible. She also read the works of Juan de Avila, at one time under suspicion by the Inquisition, who later became a trusted advisor. A question which emerges at this point, "Was she influenced by the Ignatian Exercises?" cannot be answered with certainty. Teresa was on fairly good terms with the Jesuits with only occasional fallings-out, although towards the end of her life the Jesuits at Burgos took a cool view of her manner of prayer. It is interesting that only recently has the contemplative interpretation of the *Exer-*

cises received a hearing.[7] Whatever the case, there is no doubt that her favorite work was the *Subida del Monte Sion* which, in many ways, anticipates her own work. Perhaps this attachment to Bernardino was in part due to his *Josefina,* a popular work in praise of St. Joseph, in which he attempted to correct the current pious depiction of the saint as an old man. Teresa's devotion to St. Joseph was constant and deep.

Biblical culture was quite advanced in the *Siglo de Oro.* The Bible was translated into Spanish as early as 1252 by order of King Alfonso X. In 1524, the Epistles of St. Paul were translated and, two years later, Fray Ambrosio de Montesinos translated the Gospels together with the Epistles for Enzina's *New Testament* which was later prohibited. The Psalter was immensely popular and was translated repeatedly as were Savonarola's meditations on the psalms.[8] The *Biblia de Ferrara,* which appeared in 1553, even enjoyed the scholarly pretension of being a complete translation from the Hebrew. Although many of these translations were increasingly popular, the Index of the same year, 1553, prohibited the publication and the reading of the Bible in the vernacular.

This was ostensibly a protective measure against the increasing enthusiasm of the *alumbrados* and the external peril—as it was then perceived—of Lutheranism. Theologically it was a direct attack against the private interpretation of Scripture. After all, a Bible without authorized interpretation might seem to give the reader hermeneutic *carte blanche.* Also, it was the common opinion of the time that the religious order was the substructure of the social and political domains. Control the foundational domain, the religious, and it was expected that the rest would take care of itself. In the matter of Bible translation, it is interesting to note that neither the French nor the Italian ecclesiastics agreed with the Spaniards. At the Council of Trent, two Spanish theologians, Alfonso de Castro and Cardinal Pacheco, spoke in favor of prohibition with the Italian Cardinal Madruzzi dissenting. The Council shelved the question.

In Spain where the prohibition was in effect, citations from the Bible were authorized in works with spiritual content. As was to be expected, this measure provoked some opposition and stimulated Spanish inventiveness to find ways to circumvent it. Fray Luis de

Granada, for example, wrote a veritable anthology of the New Testament in his *Guía de Pecadores* (Guide to Sinners), while Fray Luis de Leon virtually stuffed his works with scriptural citations. The works of Teresa herself are replete with biblical allusions and quotes, although her translations are often rather curious. Her close friendship with many of the scholars of the day and the generous use which even popular catechesis made of Scripture, surely led to familiarity with the major texts.

Teresa repeatedly insists that her nuns should consult a learned advisor so that they will be able to translate the truths of Holy Scripture into action. Moreover, the most important sign which testifies to the authenticity of any revelation or teaching is conformity to Scripture. Even those experiences which are recognized as indubitably certain can be accepted only insofar as they conform to Scripture and the laws of the Church. Ignorance of the Scriptures brings both spiritual and "worldly" harm in its wake. Mulling over the many reasons given against her undertaking the foundation of convents, she is told to "tell them not to follow only one part of the Scripture, to look at other parts, unless they desire to bind my hands."[9] Contemporary testimony indicates that she was considered quite a gifted interpreter of the sacred word.

Neither Teresa's use of Scripture, her language, nor her personality, are really unsettling to the contemporary reader. Actually, her literary gifts are more appreciated today than during her lifetime when her simple, folksy style was hardly the fashion. What disturbs is her familiar, almost offhand attitude towards things divine, her reports of raptures, locutions, and visions. Her post-conversion life seems to be one long dialogue with God in which the concrete world fades into a backdrop which echoes with bits and pieces of these conversations. It may strike us as being disturbingly close to psychopathology. Breuer, in a study written with Freud, states that "after all, the patron saint of hysteria, St. Teresa, was a woman of genius and great practical capacity."[10] Breuer is here taking issue with Janet's negative evaluation of hysterics based on his research with feeble-minded patients. He indicates that, contrary to Janet's opinion, people of intellect, will, character, and the highest critical genius, may be found among hysterics.

The reason that this charge has been made so much of both by admirers and detractors of the saint may be, at least in part, due to the transmutations which the term "hysteric" has undergone. Within a century or so it has moved from a Victorian term for a specifically feminine malaise to a term signifying a specific character type. Even in the more scientific area, the relatively sober interpretation of Freud can be compared to the Daliesque presentation given by Wilhelm Reich. But this is really not a substantial problem. As a psychological type, it is on the whole preferable to the computerized enthusiasm of the obsessive-complusive or the predictable evasiveness of the phobic. A few decades ago, a Spanish Carmelite, Nazario de Sta. Teresa, published an interesting volume defending the Saint against the charge.[11] Although outdated and obviously partisan, Nazario cites many relevant texts, some of which present the most radical criticisms.

It must be admitted that some of the phenomena described by Teresa are decidedly weird. One can ask: "What is to distinguish her visions of Christ from, say, Schreber's hallucinations?" How can one discern between the illness which led to her catatonic state and his hallucinatory torpor? Schreber was convinced that he was dead, decomposing, but yet in direct communication with God.[12] But if Teresa was on the path to paranoia why did she not go the whole way? Most of the *iluminados* did. To Father Francisco Gutierrez was revealed the Divine Essence in the form of an ox and Father Mendez of Seville bequeathed his followers the gifts of the Holy Spirit. Catalina de Jesus attributed the beauty of her body—itself debatable—to the practice of mental prayer.[13] These examples are pathological monstrosities of the spiritual life which occur when desire for union with God is allowed to wander at random without restraint or discipline.

The mystical element in religion seems to require tempering by historical and institutional factors. As previously indicated, Teresa insisted that spiritual gifts be measured against the rule provided by Scripture and Church discipline. A freewheeling acceptance of self is never permissible. Teresa is always far removed from egotism. The experiences which are acceptable as genuine derive their meaning as well as their verification from within the framework of traditional

Christian spirituality. It is true that the very weight of numbers, the "gravity" exercised by a substantial segment of society embracing the interior life, could well encourage a type of sensitivity conducive to aberrations. But it also can foster unusual perspicacity in dealing with such matters. Along with accounts in which evil spirits pullulate, there are many instances of practical insight: the cure of Licenciado Vidriara in Cervantes' delightful story of the same name, and John of the Cross' *dictamen* of a simpleminded nun,[14] are among the best. Teresa herself believed that most of her experiences were, in fact, divinely inspired, an opinion which was echoed after her death, with only minor and sporadic objections, by the most learned theologians of the age.

Teresa's works present us with a veritable catalog of mystical phenomena. She is far from a mere scribe as were, at least to some extent, Ángela of Foligno and Brigit of Sweden. But she was not an intellectually gifted woman in the style of Hildegard of Bingen who predicted a *tempus muliebre* which would remedy the depredations caused by the masculine gender. Rather, she was sharp, incisive, and gifted with great sensitivity. Above all else, Teresa was a nun with a clear vision of what the contemplative life should be, harking back to the legendary hermits of Mount Carmel. In spite of almost constant illness Teresa aged gracefully. She died at Alba de Tormes, probably of a massive hemorrhage. That this death was interpreted by her contemporaries as her last and greatest rapture of love serves to illustrate the optics of the times.

The Moradas

Perhaps the most important work for the comprehension of Teresa's spiritual doctrine is the *Moradas* (*The Interior Castle*) which was written in 1577 during a period of six months. At the time she was approximately sixty-two years of age. Fifteen years had elapsed since the foundation of the first Discalced Carmelite convent, San Jose, in the city of Avila. The *Life* and the *Way of Perfection* were already written, the *Foundations* nearly completed. Although she remained in harness for seven more years, most of the arduous tasks had been accomplished. The majority of her mystical experiences, at least the most spectacular ones, belonged to the past. Her spiritual life was moving to more serene heights.

The Interior Castle is one of the authentic classics of Christian spirituality, acting as guide and bellwether in the formation of the conscience of the Christian West for the past few hundred years. It was written for a special audience, though it suffers only minimally from the limitations inherent in such an approach. Though written in a language "used between women," Teresa's development of the theme leads to problems in which her language is forced to become complex if not downright speculative.

The starting point of her journey is the image of the soul as a castle made of diamond or crystal, *"todo de diamante u muy claro cristal,"* which contains many "mansions" or dwelling-places and which should be pictured as spreading outwards from the center like a palmetto.[15] Although an obvious allusion to John 14:2, many scholars have searched further afield for the source of the image, some as far as the *Kabbalah,* other more prosaic souls in the topography of Avila. Teresa herself indicates that she had a vision which presented the soul in this way which was meant to convey the soul's dignity, which, like God, exceeds the powers of the human mind. There are a multiplicity of mansions which are reduced to seven principal levels with the soul's passage through them representing the ascent to God who dwells in the seventh and highest mansion. The first three mansions pertain to the natural order, in the fourth the natural and supernatural coexist, while the last two mansions comprise the properly mystical and supernatural.

From the very beginning it is evident that the mystical life requires a scaffolding in the life of Christian piety. There are, Teresa indicates, certain necessary preconditions. Primary is self-knowledge, which is to say, the measurement of the created self in the light of the uncreated God. It is a comparison which should generate humility which is the "foundation" of the whole enterprise. Teresa states that Jesus was fond of humility "because God is Supreme Truth and to be humble is to walk in truth."[16] This is hardly a limp pseudo-virtue, a caricature in line with Nietzsche's critique of Christianity, but an extremely hard-nosed view of oneself. The soul may then enter into the castle. Teresa asks: If the castle represents the soul why do we enter where we already are? This is probably an ironical nod to the irreflexive and uncritical manner in which the majority of people accept themselves. Many souls remain stalled in the "outer courtyard" in ignorance of the castle. Others are externalized to the point of becoming like the "insects" and "vermin" which surround the castle. Teresa indicates that "spiritual books," probably referring to Osuna and Laredo, advise souls to enter into themselves.[17] Here Teresa stands between Kafka and the emerging secular method of interiorization which finds its model in Descartes' Third Meditation. But his goal is certitude not self-knowledge.

If humility is the foundation of spirituality, prayer is its gate. All prayer, be it vocal or mental, demands a minimum of attention. As Teresa states:

> A prayer in which a person is not aware of whom he is speaking to, what he is asking, who it is who is asking and of whom, I do not call prayer however much the lips may move.[18]

To address God in an unsuitable manner as if one were speaking to a slave is not prayer. With this basic preparation—the life of the sacraments and the liturgy is presupposed—the soul proceeds to enter into itself, into the first mansion. But as it is accompanied by a retinue of the courtyard denizens the soul at first fails to appreciate the beauty of the mansion it has entered. The ascent which commences at this point will bring about a progressive cleansing of spiritual sight—a traditional Platonic metaphor—together with an increasing awareness of the true worth of the soul. Teresa insists that the soul should be thought of as "spacious" and capable of far more than is usually presumed.[19]

At this point humility consists in recognizing that good works have their origin in God, not in the human soul, which is itself a paradox. Although its ground—Teresa speaks of a "fount" or "light" at the center of the soul—is unfailingly beautiful, the soul can, through sin, fall into a state which she describes as darker than darkness. If this occurs, the "inhabitants" of the castle (the senses) and its "staff" (the faculties) become blind and disordered.[20] To submerge ourselves in earthly miseries would condemn us to spiritual immobility. Teresa urges that proper self-understanding advises "to fix our eyes on Christ, our Good, and on his saints."[21] True perfection will be seen to consist in the love of God and neighbor. The more perfectly these "commandments" are kept the more perfect shall we be. This command is translated on a pragmatic level into detachment, separation from unnecessary things and activities (*"las cosas y negocios no necesarios"*) in conformity with the person's position in life.[22] This provides the foundation for even the most spectacular of mystical experiences.

The second mansion is only a modest advance over the first. Souls who have acquired self-knowledge and begun prayer are allowed to enter. Effort increases while danger decreases. Teresa compares the inhabitants of the first mansion to deaf-mutes, those of the second to persons who hear but cannot speak. The voice of God is now heard faintly and the soul is stirred to discover its true nature by means of prayer, sermons, pious readings, even through sickness and trials. The vicissitudes of life begin to lose their chaotic and meaningless appearance and coalesce into a point of departure for the awareness of God's presence. At this stage its peculiar diabolical temptation consists in attributing quasi-eternity to created things.[23] This is a nice point. It seems fitting that when God, authentic eternity, begins to make himself felt, Satan should attempt to provide temporal things with a patina of eternity so as to delude the soul. Ascetic literature usually singles out the sin of avarice as of special danger as it derives its strength from the illusory eternity attributed to money.

It may be superfluous to again mention Plato's cave-analogy but when the temptation arises to abort the entire journey, or at least to return to the first mansion, the parallel comes to mind. Somewhat reminiscent of Lull, Teresa vanquishes the temptation by appealing to the faculties of the soul. The rational faculty demonstrates that the soul is mistaken in its evaluation of worldly things through a comparison to its own highest aspirations. Faith teaches the soul that it can find fulfillment only in God while memory evidences that creature-affection ends in death and oblivion. From another perspective, the will aspires to repay the love it has received and the intellect helps the soul to realize that a better friend than God cannot be found; that outside of the castle there is neither security nor peace.[24]

The soul, Teresa indicates, is naturally directed to God, no matter how distant or how alien he seems to be. But although all men wish to experience his presence, the desire for consolations should be silenced. Although legitimate, it is subordinate to the task of conforming the human will to the divine will.[25] Nevertheless, if a consolation is experienced it should be accepted as the will of God. But here there is no place for the dilettante who transforms spirit into sensuous or aesthetic gratification, nor for mystification:

> Do not think that in what concerns perfection there is some mystery or things unknown or still to be understood, for all our good lies in perfect conformity to God's will.[26]

The third mansion is characterized by avoidance of sin, penance, periods of recollection, practical charity, modesty, and order.[27] Teresa refers to the "young man" of Matthew's Gospel 19:16, who kept the commandments but was reluctant to sell what he had and give the proceeds to the poor. He went away downhearted. This mansion is a period of both aridity in prayer and the reception of divine "favors." These experiences are given in proportion to the love of God, a love which must be exteriorized by means of deeds.[28] Teresa constantly reiterates this demand of converting aspirations into deeds even on the heights of the seventh mansion. We again encounter the *aphairesis* or detachment of the Dionysian writings but it has been defanged and domesticated—de-intellectualized—and become mere detachment from worldly things on a very practical level. A noetic operation has been converted into an ascetic norm.

The dangers which arise at this stage are many and follow a movement which bears a marked resemblance to the manic-depressive cycle and to those cases mentioned by Freud in his monograph, "Those Wrecked by Success."[29] After reaching a point of such euphoria that the soul feels itself to be "Lord of the World," a minor trial can bring down the entire house of cards. What is to be done? Admitting that she knows of no certain cure for people afflicted in this way, Teresa advises that compassion be shown them and that they should not be contradicted.[30] She suggests that as they are riding high on self-satisfied virtue, God wishes that they experience wretchedness. He withdraws his favor and this deprivation acts as a spur to self-knowledge.

It is possible for the practice of virtue to become all too moderate and reasonable. A situation resembling Kierkegaard's "moral stage" is portrayed rather ironically. A Christian of this sort is living like a virtuous pagan. His circumspection is based on fear and this tepidity impedes any spiritual progress. Teresa advises: Let love overwhelm reason and so move forward with greater speed.[31]

She spends some time discussing "interior favors" (*mercedes interiores*). They comprise both consolations (*contentos*) and spiritual delights (*gustos*). They generate love and fortitude and encourage the soul to grow in virtue and in the practice of good works. The importance of these "interior favors" is evidenced by Teresa's prefacing her analysis of them by a discussion of obedience, of the greatest importance to religious life. She goes so far as to suggest that even persons who do not belong to religious communities should, whenever possible, place themselves under obedience to a director, one who preferably is free of worldly illusion. This promotes self-knowledge and acts as an antidote to the perils of self-will. A detailed analysis of the "interior favors" is left for the following mansion.

The fourth mansion is a halfway house in which the supernatural is introduced and coexists for a time with the natural order. A change of perspective is gradually taking place. Mysticism proper commences at this stage as do mystical phenomena. The poisonous creatures which entered the castle together with the soul only rarely have access to this mansion and when they do enter, usually have a beneficial effect on the soul. Although Teresa complains of the great difficulty in explaining what occurs in the fourth mansion, she characteristically proceeds to do so with clarity and precision.

She now proceeds to discuss "interior favors" at length, distinguishing between "consolations" and "spiritual delights." There exist essential differences between the two. Consolations (*contentos*) have their origin in nature and their end in God while spiritual delights (*gustos*) have their very origin in God. Moreover, these spiritual delights are experienced in a manner superior to the way consolations are experienced. While consolations belong to the natural order, spiritual delights belong to the supernatural.[32] Continuing the theme, Teresa cites a verse from Psalm 119, *Cum dilatasti cor meum*: while spiritual delights expand the heart, consolations only serve to constrict it. Moreover, consolations may cause severe headaches, tears, and other phenomena in proportion to each individual's temperament. These affective phenomena may be experienced in previous mansions by those persons who rely on discursive thought and meditation in prayer. Teresa's advice is that it is better to love than to think much.[33] Love is not an emotion but a strong determination to please God in everything, striving not to offend him, asking for the advancement of the honor of his Son and increase of the Catholic Church.[34]

There are other physiological and psychological distinctions between the two "interior favors." Consolations are sometimes accompanied by constriction of the chest and automatic motor movements which, because of their violence, can cause nosebleeds and other physical reactions. But even these experiences—which Teresa states she has not herself experienced—are positive insofar as they tend to promote a desire to please God. Spiritual delights, which now seem to be equated with the prayer of quiet, are very different even though there is at least some confusion in the account. At any rate, in her *Life*, Teresa emphasized the passive nature of spiritual delights,[35] and this is followed up in the *Moradas* by her use of a favorite metaphor—water—to clarify the question at hand.

There are two fountains, each with a water trough. While the first is filled from a distance by means of an "artfully contrived" mechanism, the second rests directly on its source which fills the trough noiselessly.[36] The first fountain represents consolations, the second, spiritual delights. Here God produces the experience noiselessly. Peace, quiet, and sweetness flow through the soul and overflow to touch the body. This expansion of the heart comes from the deepest recesses of the soul which Teresa, following mystical tradition, calls the "center of the soul" (*el centro del alma*).[37] Spiritual delights also differ from natural experience in that the soul which experiences them understands them better than they could be understood by means of any possible explanation. The faculties are absorbed and look on astonished at what they see, *"embevidas y mirando como espantadas que es aquello."*[38] It took some time for Teresa to distinguish between the intellect and the imagination. Once she was able to do so, this enabled her to understand how she could experience simultaneously the rapid movement of the imagination and the recollection of the soul in God.[39]

The prayer of recollection usually precedes the prayer of quiet/spiritual delights. The soul addresses God and the external world and its own faculties become muted. Perhaps this prayer, as the antechamber for spiritual delights, is found on both the natural and the supernatural levels. Teresa had previously referred to this prayer of recollection as both infused and acquired—in different texts.[40] The *Moradas* indicates that it is less intense than spiritual delights and constitutes a path to a higher form of prayer.[41] Whatever the case, at this point the use of discursive reason must be set aside so that the will may rest in God. The soul, like a lamb, faintly hears the call of the Divine Shepherd. Only the activity of God who draws the soul inward can account for this prayer. It cannot be generated by the operations of the imagination or the intellect. Following Osuna, Teresa compares the process of interiorization to a hedgehog curling up, to the turtle drawing into its shell.[42]

This prayer of recollection, which in the *Moradas* texts seems to be infused, is referred to, by Teresa, as a preparation for listening, a striving to remain attentive to the work of God in the soul.[43] In the spiritual domain, an inversion of values takes place. Whoever thinks less and has less desire for activity is actually doing more. To attempt to generate this prayer through natural means would only increase aridity. Although the usual ascetic practices of penance, good deeds, and prayer should be practiced, they do not by themselves induce contemplation. The Lord should be allowed to do what he desires with the soul: "When his Majesty desires the intellect to stop, he occupies it in another way, and gives it a light so far above what we can attain, that it remains absorbed."[44] The goal is of course the prayer of quiet which is to say, at least in this context, spiritual delights.

The prayer of quiet may be compared to the fountain which grows in accordance with the water flowing into it. The soul enjoys greater freedom, is no longer constrained by the fear of hell, and believes it can do all things in God. Its faith gains intensity while, as the knowledge of God's grandeur increases, so also does humility. In the presence of spiritual delights, worldly delights are discarded. Moreover, a heightening of all the virtues takes place.[45] But in spite of these many favors Teresa surprises by comparing the soul at this stage to a "suckling babe" who is menaced by many dangers, especially those proceeding from Satan, because of the great benefit which such souls can bring to the Church.[46]

A point before continuing. It is very easy for contemporary scholarship to dismiss as an atavistic regression all references to Satan, and in Teresa there are many of them indeed. In her opinion, Satan is a very powerful, malevolent being, happily a controllable one who becomes progressively weaker as the soul ascends to God. Many of her views in this respect were traditional: devils flee from holy water, are able to deceive lay people more than religious, are at their strongest in the desert, provoke gossip, and, of course, entertain a specially virulent hatred for Discalced Carmelites.[47] But along with much folklore, whether theologically grounded or not, there is always the assurance that the good will out. The devil is a "slave" of God, its deceptions are rooted in weakness, and it is unable to penetrate into the depths of the human soul or triumph over a valiant soul.[48] The context where these speculations are found is usually practical—discussions concerning physical or psychological morbidity or the ever-present theme of "the discernment of spirits."

Nuns with weak constitutions who become even weaker because of the rigors of conventual life are never hard to find. Teresa suggest that many of these join physical weakness to interior consolations and come to believe that they are experiencing mystical favors of the highest sort. This delusion induces even greater weakness and the nun becomes convinced that she is experiencing rapture, and this, in turn, causes the "dulling" of both the physical and spiritual senses. She mentions one person who remained in a trancelike state for eight hours and was finally cured by adequate sleep, proper diet, and moderating the severity of her penances. Teresa's attitude is trenchant: "I call it being carried away in foolishness because it amounts to nothing more than wasting time and wearing down one's health."[49] In a nice play on words she states that there is more than a fine line between rapture (*arrobamiento*) and foolishness (*abobamiento*). In people with a weak imagination, sight tends to follow fantasy. Teresa was not given to naivete in her judgments.

The fifth mansion provides a discussion of the state of union which is distinguished from its counterfeit, a sort of dreamlike affair. In union, the faculties are suspended insofar as the world and even itself are concerned. The soul, Teresa states, "is like one who in every respect has died to the world, so as to live more completely in God."[50] Viewed from the outside, it has all the marks of a catatonic trance but the supernatural element may be discerned because, unlike prior experiences, the soul entertains no doubt of its authenticity. The experience transcends human categories. Nevertheless, Teresa attempts to describe it in passages which lose the smoothness of narrative to become sharp and jagged. Clearly it rises above all earthly joys and delights. The difference between the two "is like that between feeling something on the rough, outer, covering of the body and in the marrow of the bones."[51] The translation does little justice to the original Spanish which reads *"en esta grosería del cuerpo u en los tuétanos."*

But the experience is short-lived, and this suspension of the faculties does not cause any irreparable physical harm. When the soul becomes blind to itself and to the external world then God acts by imprinting his wisdom upon it. It is as impossible to doubt his presence in the soul as it is to forget the experience.[52] The Lord is able to enter the center of the soul without opening any "door" in the manner in which the risen Jesus entered the upper room to greet his disciples (Jn. 20:19). Striving to explain union further and to view it in the light of the organic development of Christian spiritual life, Teresa unfurls the well-known silkworm analogy.

According to this, silkworms are generated by small seeds the size of "little grains of pepper." Once born they nourish themselves on mulberry leaves and when full-grown settle on twigs. Then they enclose themselves in cocoons. Finally, the "fat and ugly silkworm" dies and a small lovely white butterfly is born.[53] This account represents the development of the human soul. The process begins with the practice of the virtues, the sacraments, with all else falling under the general providence of God. The house where the silkworm dies, the cocoon, represents Christ. It is by means of detachment and virtuous deeds that man allows God to become his dwelling place, his *morada*.[54] Finally the death of the old man—the silkworm—brings about the birth of the new man—the butterfly. She speaks of a preliminary union which never lasts more than half an hour during which the soul, because of the radical metamorphosis it has undergone, is unable to recognize itself.

By this experience the soul understands things which surpass its natural capacity.[55] An experience resembling this is discussed in the sixth mansion but the effects produced are different. At this stage its aftereffects include the desire to endure great trials, distaste for the world, pain because God is offended, and delight in doing his will. The true place of rest has been found. But few reach this stage of the journey, many because of their lack of charity which, even in trivial things, gnaws away at the virtues. But the soul should not lose its vigor as God has given mankind his Son to teach us the way so that we also will be perfect.[56]

Teresa distances herself from those *filósofos*, in the present case the Stoics, who counselled *apatheía*, indifference. This attitude, she remarks, is often based on impotence making a virtue of necessity.[57] After all, in the religious life only two things are indispensable: the love of God and the love of neighbor. The best indication that both are observed is the love of neighbor. The more advanced the love of neighbor, the more advanced is the love of God: "If we practice love of neighbor with great perfection we will have done everything."[58] There is another danger. To those who have arrived at this state but allow the memory of the experience to obsess them, she insists that works are desired by God and must be forthcoming. Nonetheless this is no less than an adumbration of the life of vision of the blessed albeit burdened with the flaws inherent to contingent existence.[59]

The sixth mansion is the lengthiest, most detailed, and least readable section of the *Interior Castle*, but still the most relevant for the study of mystical phenomena. It contains, as it presently reads, eleven chapters, that is, nine more than the first mansion and seven more than the seventh. It seems at first sight that Denis' dictum that the higher the contemplation the more reduced the language, has been discarded even though in actuality the greater part of this section deals with phenomena tangential to mystical union. Many pages refer to the negative aspect of the ascent, those stages of purification which John of the Cross represents by his metaphor of the dark nights of sense and spirit. For a person of Teresa's character—almost a century ago Delacroix spoke of her rich subconscious life and the exaltation of her mental images[60]—the ineffable is a challenge to her gift for indirect expression. This is one of the factors which make the pages dedicated to mystical union so attractive. Once the seventh mansion is reached Teresa becomes curiously direct and prosaic, seemingly drained of fresh metaphors, exploiting the marriage metaphor, one with which she was not fully satisfied.

The section which deals with Spiritual Betrothal (*desposorio espiritual*) begins on a low note, a laborious discussion of the obstacles and impediments to this state. They range from the seemingly trivial—gossip and praise—to the more substantial—persecution, sickness *et al.* Teresa says of herself:

> I know a person who cannot truthfully say that from the time the Lord began forty years ago to grant the favor that was mentioned, she spent even one day without pains and other kinds of suffering. . . and other great trials.[61]

The worse trials are the interior ones. She constantly had in mind—it constitutes a pervasive theme in her works—the spiritual and psychological mischief caused by misguided confessors and spiritual directors. The contemporary analogue would be the well-meaning but poorly trained psychotherapist engaged in the practice of "wild analysis." Self-doubt, misanthropy, the subjection of the understanding to the imagination also provide obstacles to the spiritual life. The latter is particularly noxious as the devil produces his deception in the imagination.[62] Still worse is a type of depression which Teresa calls "interior oppression" (*apretamiento interior*) and compares it to the suffering of the souls in hell. Grace itself is hidden.[63] But similar to depression this "tempest" can be stilled by a chance happening and, in any case, this incapacitation of the soul provides self-knowledge and is a necessary hurdle to pass if the soul is to enter the seventh mansion.[64]

Many of the phenomena discussed are considered to be ways in which God awakens the soul and leads it to its final goal. Teresa speaks of them as "delightful wounds" which come rapidly, like a thunder-clap, with the soul realizing immediately that it has been called by God. Pain and joy are both experienced with the effects producing more satisfaction than those of the prayer of quiet.[65] They are like sparks leaping from a brazier and striking the soul and cannot be counter-feited since they are clearly understood and not connected to the absorption of the faculties. They cannot even be caused by depression (*melancolía*) since the experience proceeds from the "inner part of the soul" while melancholy concocts its fantasies in the imagination.[66] This type of phenomena is often encountered in the literature of mysticism. Richard Rolle, the English mystic, speaks of mystic heat which accompanies the "new birth" of the soul.[67] And this is only one example among many possible ones.

Another way in which God awakens the soul is by means of locu-tions and these can range from single words to dialogues. The "speech" may be experienced as coming from outside the self, as taking place within consciousness, coming from the innermost part of the soul, or merely as ordinary language.[68] But discernment is required as these locutions can come from the imagination—or even from Satan—as well as from God himself. But here as elsewhere the ulti-mate criterion of authenticity is conformity with Scripture. Teresa urges the superiors of religious suffering from depression to oblige them to withdraw from prayer,[69] providing criteria to test the experiences.

First of all, authentic locutions put into effect what they state. For example, the words "Don't be distressed," are followed by a calm illumination. Secondly, the soul is left in "great quiet," in devout, peaceful recollection. Thirdly, the soul is assured of its authenticity and the words are never forgotten.[70] Satan, in his attempts at deception, will, like a true Cartesian, pronounce the words clearly and distinctly in his attempt to ape the Spirit of Truth. But the effects are different. In counterfeit locutions the soul will experience restlessness and dark-ness instead of peace and light, pride instead of humility.[71]

Spiritual betrothal is experienced when the soul is drawn out of its senses by God, i.e., when it is enraptured. Teresa insists that she is referring to the genuine article: "I mean true raptures and not the weaknesses women experience here below, for eveything seems to us to be a rapture or an ecstasy."[72] She indicates that there are several kinds of authentic rapture. One takes place when the soul is affected by a word concerning God which it hears or remembers. It brings about temporary union, although consciousness in this case does not appear to be suspended.[73] These experiences are clearly distinguishable from mere fainting or convulsions (*desmayo u parajismo*) because by their means a deep enlightenment is communicated to the soul.

Teresa also mentions "secrets," imaginative visions, and at the highest level, intellectual visions, which completely transcend human capacity of comprehension and expression.[74] In these intellectual visions the imagination is bypassed so that they contain no images. But then, how are they remembered? Admitting her own ignorance on this point, Teresa goes on to stress the great authority which they convey:

> Even if faith were not to tell it [the soul] who God is and of the obligation to believe that he is God, from that very moment it would adore him as God, as did Jacob when he saw the ladder.[75]

These experiences convey not only a knowledge which transcends discursive reason but also a certain knowledge of particulars. Teresa was at a loss to explain this until she chanced upon a happy comparison. She had visited the Duchess of Alba and, on entering into the palace, came upon a large room containing a conglomeration of things, *una baraúnda de cosas*. Although she was able to remember the room in general she was unable to focus on any given object. Something analogous to this happens to the soul as it is left with a general representation but is unable to enter into a detailed description.[76]

These experiences have interesting concomitants. They are characterized by a trancelike state with physical rigidity and anesthesia, at times muteness, faulty respiration (hyperventilation?) coldness of the hands and body, the silencing of the faculties and the senses along with unusual variations in their mode of operation. They do not last for a lengthy period. There is not total confusion. But those things which lead the will to love God are understood and they are accompanied by a state of euphoria: "The soul would desire to have a thousand lives so as to employ them all for God and that everything here on earth would be a tongue to help it praise him."[77]

Another type of rapture discussed by Teresa is the "flight of the spirit" (*vuelo del espíritu*) or "swift rapture of the spirit" (*apresurado arrebatar del espíritu*), which are much the same as those previously discussed but experienced by the soul in a different manner. The spirit seems to be carried off at a fearful speed, and, at first, there is no assurance that the experience comes from God. But in spite of this, the best course Teresa advises, is to abandon oneself to God as any resistance would be counter-productive. It must be a rather terrifying experience! Although the person is still alive no account can be given for the passage of time as the soul is alienated and seems to have been in another world where even the quality of light is different.[78]

Here there may well be some relation to the mysticism of the Transfiguration such as it was elaborated by Eastern Christianity. So much is taught by these raptures that it is impossible to translate its content into discursive reason. At this point Teresa makes an important distinction between the soul and the spirit inadvertently borrowing the Neoplatonic metaphor of the sun and its rays to represent the soul and the spirit. Although in a sense one—like the sun and its rays—the soul, remaining in its place, has the superior part, the mind, rising above it. Embarrassed by this burst of speculation, she remarks: "In a word, I don't know what I'm saying."[79]

Teresa counters the view, very much in the Dionysian tradition, that meditation on the mysteries of Christ's humanity are to be eschewed on this elevated spiritual plane. This view is paraphrased as follows: "when souls have already passed beyond the beginning stages it is better for them to deal with things concerning divinity and flee from corporeal things."[80] This, she states, is sound advice for "angelic spirits" but not for human beings who are the companions in arms of those beings who, possessing a mortal body, were able to do great things for God. To discard the humanity of Christ is to discard the one guide to the higher levels of spiritual life. Whoever does discard him will either regress or progress no further. Possibly having the scriptural tergiversations of the *iluminados* in mind in this respect she adds:

They will say that another meaning is given to these words. I don't know about those other meanings, I have gotten along very well with this one that my soul feels to be true.[81]

Although Teresa concedes that a soul in perfect contemplation may find it difficult to engage in discursive meditation concerning the life of Christ, he always remains the soul's companion and the "bridge" between the human and divine. In addition, though the point of departure for contemplation may be merely a thought or an image, a leap then takes place which obliterates discursive thought and in which the mysteries are understood in a more perfect manner.[82]

The eighth chapter of the sixth mansion continues the discussions of visions some of which—those experienced through bodily sight—were never experienced by Teresa herself. More perplexing are the "imaginative" and "intellectual" visions, especially when she uses an example such as the following to illustrate the latter: sensing that Jesus, although not perceptible through vision, is next to her. Nevertheless, she insists that these visions manifest their authenticity, last for many *days*, and are very helpful in acquiring habitual recollection of God.[83] Imaginative visions are lower in status but may be more beneficial than the intellectual visions as they are more in conformity with human nature. She gives as example visions of Jesus' humanity, a "glorious image" which is received in consciousness and imprinted on the imagination.[84] This image is experienced as living, as speaking to the soul, and even as revealing "secrets." Seen by the inner eye, the experience can be awesome: "almost every time God grants this favor the soul is in rapture, for in its lowliness it cannot suffer so frightening a sight."[85] Whatever goes beyond the capacity of the imagination and intellect as these experiences do is very hard to come to terms with.

But there are other ways in which God communicates with the human soul that are even more elevated but less dangerous to its well-being. Teresa speaks of a suspension which comes suddenly while a person is at prayer and which communicates *grandes secretos*. They seem to be seen in God himself. The whole of creation may be viewed from the vantage point of God. They are authentic intellectual visions,[86] and similar to the experiences described by John of the Cross. Although they bear a superficial resemblance to the intellectualistic visions described by Spinoza among others, they should be distinguished from these speculative flights "to our dear country" in that they are given by God and are not the end result of a process of thought.

These experiences, far from satisfying the soul, only add to its misery as the person begins to realize the measure in which God should be loved and how very distant it is from this goal.[87] The symptoms become so distressing that even the possibility of death cannot be discarded. The body becomes disjointed, the heartbeat becomes faint, and great weakness ensues to the extent that "for three or four days afterward one feels great suffering and doesn't even have the strength to write."[88] A strange solitude pervades the soul as everything short of God is incapable of providing it with satisfaction. All earthly things seem to be "shadows,"[89] and a sense of unreality pervades the soul. This malaise increases to the point of such intense distress that it can be alleviated only by God himself.

Situated in a realm outside the everyday world, subject to dangerous attacks of both pain and joy which seem to flow into each other, the soul is living a life superior to itself, hidden within the divine life. This life, at its highest, is called Spiritual Marriage. The soul is taken into the seventh mansion as into "another heaven,"[90] a state of union in which a deeper understanding of the favors it has been given is granted, by means of an intellectual vision of the Holy Trinity. That which was previously known by faith is now apprehended, "seen," but neither with the eyes of the body nor of the soul. In this vision the three Persons of the Trinity communicate themselves to the soul and speak to it, "explaining" the words of the Johannine Gospel 14:23:

> If anyone loves me he will keep my word
> and my Father will live in him
> and we shall come to him
> and make our home with him.

Although the divine presence is dwelling in the soul, it becomes occupied more than ever with things that belong to the service of God instead of being absorbed in contemplation.[91] The Trinitarian presence no longer has the urgency nor the clarity which it possessed before. It becomes a "companionship" which prompts the soul to advance in perfection.

The distinction between the soul and the spirit, previously mentioned, seems to have intrigued Teresa who again discusses it, now employing the Martha/Mary symbolism. In this analogy, Martha represents the lower sensibility—the self of the everyday world—while Mary represents the transcendent self which permanently enjoys the presence of God. The spirit is found within the soul though at times they seem to function in different ways. While the spirit is recollected in God, the soul is victimized by the hurly-burly of the imagination and the external world. It is the mission of Mary, Teresa insists, to help Martha correct the instability of the imagination caused by original sin so as to eventually produce "good works."

Spiritual marriage takes place in the very center of the soul, the seventh *morada* where God himself dwells. Knowledge and joy are experienced to such an extreme degree that Teresa speaks of a revelation of the glory of heaven.[92] The spirit is now made one with God. While Spiritual Betrothal was compared to the joining of two candles in which wick, flame, and wax become one but may be later separated, Spiritual Marriage is compared to a small stream which enters and merges with the sea.[93] The pantheistic overtones are clear but more apparent than real with the scriptural ground encountered in 1 Cor. 6:17 and Phil. 1:21. The latter text is given by Teresa in her own version: *"Mi qui bivere Christus es mori lucrum."*[94]

Here again the assurance of its authenticity is immediately given in consciousness and, with the passage of time, in the beneficial effects on a person's life. The soul is apodictically certain that "there is someone in the interior depths [of the soul] who gives life to life, and is the source of these manifestations."[95] Teresa insists that God's words become deeds in us, principles of activity which transform the souls who hear them by disengaging them from their love of creatures. Though the soul is not assured of salvation, it rests at peace. The senses, the faculties, and the affects now reside on the periphery of the soul and are unable to enter into its center.[96] The positive effects in the practical sphere will continue to manifest themselves.

Among these Teresa lists forgetfulness of self, a great desire to suffer for God, and the realization that everything God does is good. Perhaps a spiritual version of the real is the ideal. Also intense joy when suffering persecution, special love for the persecutors, little fear of death, great detachment, and desire for solitude and work advantageous to others. At this point raptures cease while inner agitation and spiritual aridity notably diminish.[97] God is teaching the soul in silence, and this is compared to the building of Solomon's Temple (1 Kgs. 6:7) where no sound of hammer, pick, or any tool, was heard. The clamor and distress of many of the experiences cataloged previously, running the spectrum from auditions to ecstasies, were due, at least in part, to the weaknesses of the soul, not its strength. This is why they cease when the soul is strengthened and its capacity increased. But the end of Spiritual Marriage as of the lesser gifts is still good works, "always good works."[98] Teresa advises her daughters: "let us desire and be occupied in prayer not for the sake of our enjoyment but so to have the strength to serve."[99]

Martha is joined to Mary, the soul is joined to the spirit, in the task of salvation. Whatever the case, it is love that really counts, not the magnitude of the task at hand. And at the end of the journey the soul attains "true peace" which is a superior state of integration in which it overcomes past weaknesses and grows in proportion to the spirit of God who is transforming it. Teresa states that this is the peace of Christ, a peace which the world cannot give (Jn. 14:27).

The final chapter is anticlimactic. The gap between experience and explanation, which has been widening progressively, becomes an abyss. The writer is faced with the choice of lapsing into silence or returning to the pedestrian world. Teresa follows the latter option. In a pious, somewhat moralistic afterthought—though not devoid of her usual piquancy—she admonishes her nuns not to build castles in the air:[100] a perennial temptation among the more foolhardy of her admirers. But only a perfect wretch would not sympathize with this self-styled *pobre miserable* who asks for our prayers at the end of the book.

Whatever the final evaluation may be concerning the literary and speculative merit of the *Interior Castle*, its value to the literature of mysticism is assured. The veritable maelstrom of mystical phenomena discussed, no matter how bizarre, are passed through the filter of Christian dogma and pious belief. The solidity of Teresa's faith gives credence to those disturbing alien melodies. It may be well to recall the comments of the Jesuit, Father Ribera, when attempting to correct the well-meaning but unfortunate job of editing the *Interior Castle* attempted by her friend and fellow Carmelite, Fray Gracián:

> And I ask out of charity anyone who reads this book to reverence the words and letters formed by so holy a hand and try to understand her correctly... Even if you do not understand, believe that she who wrote it knew better and that the words cannot be corrected unless their meaning is fully understood.[101]

Epilogue

Teresa's role in the development of Christian spirituality is difficult to ascertian with precision, although her work and that of John of the Cross can reasonably be considered the last classics in the literature of mysticism. In many ways she is far more at ease in the modern world than her associate in the Carmelite Reform. Less inclined to the speculative than many of her predecessors, she is as firmly rooted in the Christian faith and, lacking their sometimes heavy pace, has yet to be relegated to the status of a religious museum piece. She seldom bores or cloys, is readable, and usually understandable to the moderately educated. The many superb passages encountered in her works make her repetitiousness—for which she quite rightly faults herself—simply a minor flaw. When clarity of expression is joined to practical insight and put into the service of her perverse sense of humor, the result is impressive indeed. Because of this she remains, even today, the inspiration if not the source of much of the best work on the spiritual life.

To a world which senses, quite rightly, that many of the dear things have been lost, not the least of which are those related to spiritual concerns, she is one of the few voices who command attention. Her presence is felt in many fields of human endeavor. Her works have generated general enthusiasm in the speculative mind from Pascal to Bergson and beyond. Leibniz specifically recognized his debt to Teresa for the proposition that the soul should conceive all things as if only

God and itself existed in the world.[102] It is intriguing to find her aphorism, Dionysian roots and all, enjoying continued existence in the world of the mathematization of nature with the mansions impinging upon the monadology.

The life and work of Teresa has been a mine, perhaps all too often explored, for psychological spelunkers, even before the time of William James. Pierre Janet, Henri Delacroix, and Jean L' Hermitte were among the many who contributed insights. Popular literature has embroidered the theme of the Saint from Avila in works which range from the perceptive to exercises in treacle. Books on prayer inspired by her doctrine and commentaries on her work continue to be published with some regularity. Her lively but undistinguished poetry has found many imitators. More important still, her life and works continue to inspire the best human aspirations, making a persuasive case for the hidden life, a life which today is all too often ignored.

Perhaps the greatest disservice to her is done by those reductionist critics who transform the feisty Castilian nun into a cipher in a psychiatric casebook or into a model of saccharine piety, endlessly mouthing sententious platitudes. Both versions fail to take into account her toughness, resiliency, and great practical ability. A person who compares the spiritual life to a game of chess in which the object is to checkmate God,[103] and who lived her life accordingly, should be spared caricature. Teresa's God lived in the seventh mansion but could also be found among the pots and pans. His love pursued her everywhere. A short time before her death Teresa and her nuns were trapped by a flood in the Discalced foundation at Burgos. The convent was in peril and buffeted on all sides. When neighbors asked the Carmelite community to leave by boat, Teresa declined. When told of their predicament, the Archbishop is said to have exclaimed: "Leave Teresa of Avila alone, she has a safe-conduct to depart with whatever she wants."[104] This mixture of awe, humor, and a touch of irony may well be a fitting commentary for such a unique life.

A few years ago, a volume appeared to commemorate the proclamation of Saint Teresa as Doctor of the Church on September 27, 1970.[105] Prominent theologians and others contributed articles, brief pieces, and letters. Most of the contributions ran true to form in conformity with Christian thought under the aegis of Heidegger. Karl Rahner interpreted the proclamation as the occasion for the posing of several questions concerning the relation between Christian and natural mysticism.[106] Truhlar here viewed mysticism as an experiential buttressing for a crumbling rationalism,[107] while Vandenbroucke suggested that the mystic is a witness to the immanence of God, an antidote against the "scandal" of evil, the apparent absence of Providence.[108] Schillebeeckx, for his part, viewed the mystic as the prophet of God's presence, a presence which is lived paradoxically by us in the form of the human experience of absence.[109] Common to all these views was the accent on the here and now, the this-worldly.

From the silence of the cloister, Giovanna della Croce echoes their views by stating that the mystical problem is, above all else, an eminently human problem.[110] But she veers in another direction by stressing that the specific Teresian charism is not prophetic, as many claim, but rather is concerned with the fecundity of the contemplative life vis-à-vis the spiritual growth of the entire Mystical Body.[111] Teresa not only imitates biblical models but is obliged to relive in herself the revealed word on a spiritual-mystical level. Giovanna della Croce insists on the imperative need for a theology of *transcendence* lived in total openness to love. Only in this way, she urges, can the Mystical Body obtain the vitality which is indispensable for it to affirm itself in the world today.[112] This spiritual realism, in which immanence and transcendence coalesce in the human world and the other-worldly energizes the this-worldly, is very much in the spirit of Teresa. Both the Saint and her present-day disciple know full well that *solo Dios basta*, and that the discovery of God in the soul is paralleled by the discovery of the soul in God.

Notes

[1]*Antología General de Menendez Pelayo,* ed. by J. M. Sanchez, (Madrid: BAC, 1956), vol. I, No. 2044, (p. 621).

[2]*Ibid.,* vol. II, pp. 1195-1197.

[3]*Ibid.,* vol. II, p. 1197.

[4]For the first years of the Discalced Carmelite Reform refer to Fr. Silverio de Sta. Teresa, *Historia del Carmen Descalzo,* (Burgos: El Monte Carmelo, 1935-1949), 15 vols. For a very schematic presentation, E. Allison Peers, *Handbook to the Life and Times of St. Teresa and St. John of the Cross,* (London: Burns and Oates, 1954). For a thorough treatment of the life of St. Teresa, Efren de la Madre de Dios and Otger Steggink, *Tiempo y Vida de Sta. Teresa,* (Madrid: BAC, 1968). More compact is Efren de la Madre de Dios, *Teresa de Jesús,* (Madrid: BAC, 1981).

[5]Efren and Otger, *op. cit.,* pp. 4-6.

[6]For a brief summary of the *devotio moderna,* Dom Francois Vanden-broucke, *The Spirituality of the Middle Ages,* (London: Burns and Oates, 1968), vol. II, pp. 428-446.

[7]Refer to William A. M. Peters, *The Spiritual Exercises of St. Ignatius,* (Jersey City: The Program to Adapt the Spiritual Exercises, 1967).

[8]Jean Vilnet, *La Biblia en la Obra de San Juan de la Cruz,* trans. M. de Lizuso, (Buenos Aires: Editions Desclée de Brouwer, 1953), esp. pp. 15-28.

[9]Basic text used·is *Obras Completas de Sta. Teresa,* intro. and notes by Efren de la Madre de Dios and Otger Steggink, (Madrid: BAC, 1967). English trans. of *Moradas* by K. Kavanaugh and O. Rodriguez, *Teresa of Avila: The Interior Castle,* (New York: Paulist Press, 1979). As there are certain inconsistencies between the text given in the *Obras Completas* and the English translation, the page number of the latter will also be provided. For Teresa's evaluation of Scripture refer to *Vida* 13, 16-17; 25, 13; 32, 17; 33, 5; 40, 1; *Cuentas de conciencia* 16a, *Moradas* 6, 3, 4; 7, 3, 13; *Fundaciones* 30, 1, *et al.*

[10]Josef Breur and Sigmund Freud, *Studies on Hysteria,* standard edition. *The Complete Works of Sigmund Freud,* ed. James Strachey, (London: The Hogarth Press, 1971), vol. II, p. 232.

[11]Nazario de Sta. Teresa, *La Psicología de Sta. Teresa,* (Avila: Estudios del Colegio Filosofico "La Santa," 1950), esp. pp. 17-30.

[12]Sigmund Freud, *Notes on a Case of Paranoia,* standard edition, vol. XX, pp. 3-84.

[13]Such esoterica is described by Marcelino Menendez Pelayo, *Historia de los Heterodoxos Españoles,* (Madrid: BAC, 1956), vol. II, pp. 169-233.

[14]In Crisógono's life of John of the Cross a sober analysis of a case of depression (melancholia) follows a shocking account of an exorcism. Crisógono de Jesus, *Vida y Obras de San Juan de la Cruz*, (Madrid: BAC, 1960), pp. 117-124.

[15]*Moradas*, I, 1, 1, (p. 42).

[16]*Ibid.*, I, 2, 8-9, (42-43); VII, 4, 8, (190-191); VI, 10, 7, (165).

[17]*Ibid.*, I, 1, 5, (37).

[18]I, 1, 7, (38).

[19]I, 2, 8, (42).

[20]I, 2, 4, (41).

[21]I, 2, 11, (44).

[22]I, 2, 14; 17, (45; 47).

[23]II, 1, 3, (49-50).

[24]II, 1, 4, (50).

[25]II, 1, 7-8, (51-2).

[26]II, 1, 8, (52).

[27]III, 1, 5, (57).

[28]III, 1, 7, (58-9).

[29]"Some Character Types Met With in Psycho-Analytic Work," standard edition, vol. XIV, pp. 316-318; 324-325; 331.

[30]*Moradas* III, 2, 2, (60).

[31]III, 2, 7-8, (62-3).

[32]IV, 1, 4, (68-9).

[33]IV, 1, 7, (70).

[34]*Idem*.

[35]*Vida*, 14, 15.

[36]*Moradas*, IV, 2, 2-4, (73-4).

[37]IV, 2, 5, (74-5).

[38]IV, 2, 6, (75).

[39]IV, 1, 11, (71-72).

[40]*Vida*, 14, 15; *Camino de Perfección* 28, 29.

[41]*Moradas*, IV, 3, 8, (81).

[42]IV, 3, 3, (78-9).

[43]IV, 3, 4, (79).

[44]IV, 3, 5-6, (79-80).

[45]IV, 3, 9, (81-2); IV, 3, 12, (84).

[46]IV, 3, 10, (82-3).

[47]*Vida*, 31, 1-10. *Meditaciones sobre los Cantares* 2, 30; *Camino de Perfección*, 12, 6-7; *Cuentas de conciencia* 34a, 1; *Cartas* 19, 5; 266 *et al.*

[48] *Vida,* 25, 15; 15, 10; *Moradas* V, 1, 5, (88); VI, 6, 8, (140-1).

[49] VI, 3, 11, (83-4).

[50] V, 1, 3, (86-7).

[51] V, 1, 6, (88).

[52] V, 1, 8, (89).

[53] V, 2, 2, (91-2).

[54] V, 2, 4-6, (92-3).

[55] V, 4, 4, (103-4).

[56] V, 3, 7, (100).

[57] *Idem.*

[58] V, 3, 9, (100-1).

[59] V, 3, 11, (101-2); V, 4, 11, (106-107).

[60] Cited by Evelyn Underhill, *Mysticism,* (New York: E. P. Dutton, 1961), p. 108.

[61] *Moradas,* VI, 1, 7, (111).

[62] V, 3, 10, (101).

[63] VI, 1, 9-11, (112-3).

[64] VI, 1, 10, (113); VI, 1, 15, (114-5).

[65] VI, 2, 2, (115-6).

[66] VI, 2, 7, (118).

[67] Cited by Underhill, *op. cit.,* p. 193.

[68] *Moradas,* VI, 3, 1, (119).

[69] VI, 3, 3, (119-120).

[70] VI, 3, 5-8, (120-2).

[71] VI, 3, 16-17, (124-5).

[72] VI, 4, 2, (126-7).

[73] VI, 4, 3, (127).

[74] VI, 4, 5, (128).

[75] VI, 4, 6, (128).

[76] VI, 4, 8, (129-30).

[77] VI, 4, 15, (132).

[78] VI, 5, 7, (135-6); VI, 5, 1, (133).

[79] VI, 5, 9, (136-7).

[80] VI, 7, 5, (145).

[81] VI, 7, 6, (145-6).

[82] VI, 7, 11, (148).

[83] VI, 8, 3, (151-2).

[84] VI, 9, 3, (156-7).

[85] VI, 9, 4-5, (157).

[86]VI, 10, 3, (163-4).

[87]VI, 11, 1, (166).

[88]VI, 11, 4-8, (167-9).

[89]VI, 11, 8, (169).

[90]VII, 1, 3, (173-4).

[91]VII, 1, 6-8, (174-5).

[92]VII, 2, 4, (178).

[93]VII, 2, 5, (179).

[94]VII, 2, 6, (179).

[95]VII, 2, 6, (179-80).

[96]VII, 2, 11, (181-2).

[97]VII, 3, 2-12, (183-7).

[98]VII, 4, 6-7, (189-90).

[99]VII, 4, 12, (192).

[100]VII, 4, 18, (194).

[101]*Interior Castle,* pp. 201-202, note 2.

[102]Refer to Jacques Chevalier, *Historia del Pensamiento,* trans. by J. A. Miguez, (Madrid: Aguilar, 1967), vol. II, pp. 647-664.

[103]*Camino* [Escorial], 24, 1

[104]Efren and Otger, *Vida y Tiempo,* p. 737.

[105]*Teresa de Jesus: Doctora de la Iglesia,* (Madrid: Revista de Espiritualidad, 1970).

[106]Karl Rahner, "La experiencia personal de Dios más apremiante que nunca." *Idem.,* pp. 22-25.

[107]Vladimir Truhlar, "Contemplación en medio del mundo." *Idem.,* pp. 25-27.

[108]Francois Vandenbroucke, "El místico experimenta lo que nosotros creemos." *Idem.,* pp. 27-31.

[109]E. Schillebeeckx, "Profetas de la presencia viva de Dios." *Idem.,* pp. 31-34.

[110]Giovanna della Croce, "Peculiaridades de la mística teresiana" *Idem.,* pp. 174-192, esp. p. 175. The *Informatio Patroni,* also presented in this volume (pp. 83-160), is useful though not in a scholarly way.

[111]*Ibid.,* p. 176.

[112]*Ibid.,* pp. 178-182; 189-190.

Epilogue

"Let us fly to our beloved Fatherland." This seems to be the perennial cry of the mystic. Plotinus believed that Ulysses' escape from Circe and Calypso represented the attempt to ascend to the Fatherland on high.[1] Proclus interpreted Ithaca as the mystical port to which the hero is destined to return.[2] Clement of Alexandria views Ulysses binding himself to the mast to avoid the enchantment of the Sirens as the Christian who defeats temptation by binding himself to the wood of the Cross.[3] He takes a dim view of Ulysses' rejection of immortality so as to return to Ithaca, insisting that the Fatherland is above not below. The metaphor takes on a different meaning when it is inserted within the backdrop of Christian belief.

The present study is merely an attempt to discuss one of these "flights" to the Fatherland found in the history of Christian spirituality. Beginning with the Neoplatonic ascent through negations of Pseudo-Denis—perhaps closer to that of Proclus than is generally believed—it ends with Teresa's account of the elevation of the soul to the seventh mansion. Ramón Lull's efforts to borrow from Islamic religious practice and domesticate it within the boundaries of his Art, as well as Bonaventure's speculative pilgrimage to God are also considered. With these examples the principal varieties of mystical speculation, from the rank intellectualistic to the affective, have been touched on, at least peripherally, as has the spectrum of mystical experience.

The brief historical survey which accompanies each study is intended to bring to the surface those themes which influenced the age as well as those which continue to provoke interest. Denis without the Desert Fathers, Bonaventure without the Eternal Gospel and the Franciscan *Zelanti,* Lull separated from the Mendicant polemic with the Jews, Teresa isolated from the age of Philip II, would be, at best, hollow shells. The writer of mystical literature, as all humanity, is composed of flesh and blood, and viewing historical circumstances allows the reader to make the necessary cultural adjustments. Moreover, it allows at least a passing nod to other mystical writers, pseudo-mystics, theologians, philosophers, and other assorted *illuminati* and fringe-persons. It provides the study with texture and depth.

The selection of Pseudo-Denis, Bonaventure, Ramón Lull, and Teresa of Avila, is arbitrary, though not extravagantly so. It may even seem that they were chosen to reflect a rather arbitrary picture of the history of the literature of mysticism. Here, mystical speculation begins with the hyper-intellectualism of Denis and slowly rids itself of Neoplatonic excrescences until it becomes comfortably ensconced within the world of Christian piety with Teresa of Avila. This is a convenient schema and has the pedagogical advantages of clarity and logical cohesion to recommend it. But it has the unfortunate disadvantage of being false. Pious spirituality and mysticism predates Bonaventure, and intellectualistic mysticism runs alongside Lull in the person of Meister Eckhart. Isabel of Schonau and Gertrude belong to the same world as Hugo and Richard of St. Victor. Bernard is at least as "pious" as Teresa while Catherine of Siena gives detailed descriptions of the Spiritual Marriage some two hundred years before the composition of the *Moradas*. In the fourteenth century, Meister Eckhart returns to Pseudo-Denis for his inspiration and becomes even more intellectualistic because of the long-range influence exercised by Aristotle. His abstruse speculations become muted and lovely in the Rhineland mystics who prepare the way for Teresa and John of the Cross.

To end the study with Teresa may well appear to be unjustified and the absence of contributions from the Orthodox, Anglican, and Protestant camps a serious flaw. The facile rejoinder would be that in cases of this sort a *prise-de-distance* is necessary and that a few centuries are hardly sufficient to provide the required objectivity. In spite of the summary negative evaluation of mystical literature after the sixteenth century, a good argument can be made that the fragmentation of Christianity, the wars of religion, and long-term enmities militated against the genre. In addition, the noisy, chattering, open world of modernity is hardly productive of the life of solitude, either physical or psychological, which is conducive to the spiritual life. Other interests, horizontal in nature, tend to still the call from the Fatherland. A worldly spirituality, however necessary and praiseworthy in other ways, falls short in this regard.

Furthermore, it is a fairly safe generalization to state that the literature of mysticism after Teresa and John of the Cross, never quite recovers its intensity and profundity. There seems to be a failure of both spiritual and literary nerve. On the Catholic side one can mention Francis de Sales, Cardinal Berulle, perhaps even Madame Guyon, but there is something closeted and nice, even petty, about them. When an impressive figure is seen, such as Souer Elisabeth de la Trinité, it is the heroism of her life which impresses, not her writings.[4] There are, of course, tangential figures, well-intentioned but slightly ludicrous, who only serve to muddy the waters. Maria de Agreda, confidant of Philip IV of Spain, a sort of Boswell of Jesus and Mary, who catalogs every (apocryphal) event of their earthly lives in her encyclopedic *Mística Ciudad de Dios*. Or more recently, the peripatetic nun, Sr. Josefa Menendez, whose chief merit seemed to consist in a form of spectacular gymnastics by which she was transported from place to place with lightning rapidity and great confusion.

There are, of course, some second thoughts, which may someday lead to an additional study. Insofar as non-Catholic Christianity is concerned, Francis Rous' *Mystical Marriage* could have been included as an expression of traditional mystical speculation. To a lesser degree, Arndt's *True Christianity*, the Cambridge Platonists, and the usually superb, never commonplace poetry of Donne, Herbert, Vaughn, Traherne, and Crashaw. The gigantic figure of Jacob Boehme remains ambivalent. This bizarre mixture of the *Kabbalah*, Renaissance Platonism, and Paracelsus can be classified as Christian only hesitantly as his contemporaries learned to their displeasure. Nevertheless, his *Aurora* has intimations of Meister Eckhart, and such diverse characters as Henry More, Newton, and Charles I of England were his admirers. His presence was felt by Hegel and Schelling. It would still be difficult to place him within the confines of Christian mysticism and still less within the modest scope of the present study.

Some regrettable omissions were due simply to the vicissitudes of time, memory, knowledge, and opportunity. The absence of representatives of Eastern Christianity is certainly unfortunate. Men such as Simeon the New Theologian, Gregory Palamas, and even Seraphim of Sarov, spiritual movements such as Hesychasm, practices such as the Jesus-prayer, have much to teach us. Closer to home, the exclusion of Gregory, Augustine, and Bernard is regrettable. The delightful passage in the *Confessions*[5] where Augustine and Monica ascend to contemplation through dialogue alone deserves a volume. To bring in John of the Cross as a lengthy footnote to Pseudo-Denis is scarcely to do him justice.

So much for self-flagellation! These few pages did succeed in covering a fairly representative selection of men and women who contributed to the literature of mysticism and had a marked influence on both their world and posterity. All four left a definite imprint on the secular world. Philosophy, literature, and logic are in their debt as well as theology and spirituality. They exercised a pervasive if subliminal influence on the obscure corners of the human psyche. From the human point of view most are sympathetic; all, to some extent, flawed. That treasure may be found in clay is consubstantial to the Christian message.

Charles Péguy, who himself had been accused of mystical aspirations, once stated that Christianity in the modern world has the tragic beauty of a woman who alone holds a fortress intact for her Lord.[6] He viewed all Christians as *miles Christi*, soldiers of Christ, holding off a flood of infidelity which threatens on all sides. Is he right? At this point the mystics enter the scene. They represent the highest human tone, the goal to which all Christians aspire, and provide the standard against which any judgment regarding ultimate questions should be measured. If, as Péguy believed, in the twentieth century there are no fixed frontiers between good and evil, that the frontier is everywhere, then knowledge of the works of the mystics and the assimilation of their spirit becomes an urgent task. In a world which may seem to be closed to the voice of God, the mystics summon humanity to the true Fatherland.

Notes

[1] *Enneads,* I, 6, 8.

[2] *In Plat. Parm. V,* cited by Jean Pepin, "The Platonic and Christian Ulysses," *Neoplatonism and Christian Thought,* ed. D. J. O'Meara, (Norfolk: Int. Society for Neoplatonic Studies, 1982), pp. 3-23., esp. p. 5; 235, note 15.

[3] *Protrepticus,* XII, 118, 1-4. See Pepin, *op. cit.,* p. 237, note 37.

[4] The extent of her writings is still uncertain.

[5] *Confessions,* IX, 10.

[6] Charles Péguy, *Basic Verities,* Fr./Eng. bilingual edition, (New York: Pantheon Books, 1948), pp. 172-177.